AN INTERFACE FOR A FRACTAL LANDSCAPE

ED STECK

Ugly Duckling Presse, 2019

An Interface for a Fractal Landscape
© Ed Steck, 2019

ISBN 978-1-946433-01-5
First Edition, First Printing, 2019

Ugly Duckling Presse
The Old American Can Factory
232 Third Street #E-303
Brooklyn, NY 11215
www.uglyducklingpresse.org

Distributed by SPD/Small Press Distribution, Inpress Books (UK),
and Raincoast Books (Canada) via Coach House Books

Books printed offset and bound at Thomson-Shore
Design and typesetting by Doormouse with the author
The type is Adobe Garamond Pro and Courier New

The publication of this book was made possible, in part, by a grant from
the National Endowment for the Arts, and the continued support of
the New York State Council on the Arts.

TABLE OF CONTENTS

on
"Entering virtual nature
I walk the #fractal landscape
I sketch on screenshot textures
                    digital
                    nature

body / nature
old body / nature
Walking fractal landscape wow I want to
                                    laugh here
an I the first biological lifeform to laugh
                                in virtual nature?

I laughed ha ha

I thought it's be louder

bush

orange grove
ferns moving in swamp

LIGHT_SRC_VAL=39875

A fractal landscape is composed of an infinite arrangement of triangles forming a recursive spiraling loop.

Fractal landscapes first appeared as prominent terrain support for both virtual and organic life immediately following the collapse of sustainable physical realms. With significant physical-to-simulated transfer advancements, the need for bodily habitation to sustain life was no longer necessary.

As physical bodies went into cryo-metastasis, the assemblage of filtered microdata from the body was integrated into the real-time chronology of the virtual terrain in the form of an adapted biological entry enablement configuration, or, simply, a user.

Organic lifeforms were free to shed bodily occupation and embrace the autonomy of virtual existence. Initially, the integration of organic lifeforms was a flawless process. Users freely interacted with faux-natural terrain features and coded flora and fauna, generated by an algorithm designed to create symmetry between users and landscape.

In short, organic lifeform existence on a fractal landscape was seemingly a utopic, autonomous one purely platformed around user experience as a foundation for existence. However, the rapid influx of users began to compromise the stability of the virtual terrains, often resulting in irreparable user integration error.

To ease user error, archival crawler units were introduced. The use of archival crawlers enabled with synesthesia modules has recently come under significant scrutiny in terrain generation circles.

In one instance, an archival crawler unit, cataloging terrain features on an outmoded server, experienced data sickness due to a corrupt synesthesia module.

The crawler's performance weakened under the failed implementation of its own devices: incomplete exploratory drive install, faulty drawbridge-style destiny, weak beam production and impact.

Beam impact conducted surplus intake of known data and unknown data.

Instead of functioning in a beam, the impact arrowed out, absorbing fractal configurations of all known and unknown terrain features of the fractal landscape including both programmed and anomalous extensions of mountains, rivers, canyons, lakes, atmosphere, forests, and plains.

Additionally, unknown to the archival crawl conductors at the time, the unit cataloged the entirety of the known and unknown flora and fauna on the outmoded server hosting the fractal landscape.

Due to this massive absorption of information, large enough for an entire archival program, the single unit exhibited abnormal synesthetic reaction functions

in response to the unknown cataloged features and items.

The crawl is now considered to be one of the most controversial catalogs of outmoded servers to ever occur as it was accused of manipulating findings to cover up the appearances of organic matter on a virtual terrain.

The physical dimension is a pre-programmed model designed to test the possibility of restructuring organic responses through an interface for a fractal landscape.

The fractal landscape is a procedurally generated world constructed through a linked catalog of archived user-generated modules.

The archived user-generated modules are indexed as tags and then applied to individual interactions on the fractal landscape: a user pings objects, memories, or experiences to specific

time intervals and site sectors on the fractal landscape.

The terrain features of the fractal landscape are generated from pre-existing user experiences of nature that were once cataloged on a separate outmoded server.

The user experiences are redacted to remove all signifiers of that particular individual lived moment; only objects remain: river, mountain, grass, rock, elm tree, pine tree, moose.

The goal of the fractal landscape is to virtually replicate a model of organic existence interfacing with a procedurally generated fractal landscape in hopes of porting all of the cataloged interactions from an outmoded server to an active server.

The preservation of the cataloged interactions of an interface for a fractal landscape on an active server would enable all virtual tenancy the opportunity to feel how organic life experienced being and nature.

Into the opening, the horizon's end bends into itself, creating a connected curving loop.

There is a moment in the loop when the surrounding landscape caves in on itself, into the intersection of association and materialization.

The associative memory blends with the living memory at this point, molding a physical material able to be experienced as the source would experience it.

The blend enables initiation of memory, an authentic experience, in a landscape where all authenticity has become remote and compromised.

Under the density of looming air, submersible weight allows faux-breathing patterns for the anti-vessel.

The simulation of oxygen flow calms the disembodied cognitive processing of the archival crawler unit.

The calm allows it to continue functioning beyond its body, to roam the environment created after its dissipation —an environment of management constantly examining pulled associative objects.

A fractal landscape is processed from a vertical organization of user-generated natural spaces.

It is tiled in its whiteness.

It is blank, formable, and consistent.

It can be remotely structured and embodied by an index of archival crawler units linked by user-generated tags.

Archival crawler units can enter the fractal landscape to manage, modify, and fabricate environments in development with the matter encompassed within.

The systematic structure of the fractal landscape reveals accessible sectors designated for the control of the archival crawler unit through communication, simulation, and regression.

A panel of information parallels a panel of simulation in an analogous alternate realm.

Proportional interdependency in the fractal landscape is not a form of control but, rather, an observation and an archive.

Control is the freedom of trust between the archival crawler unit and the matter disclosed in the accessible sectors of the fractal landscape.

Individual fractal landscape sectors contain multitudes of effects for prospective growth of both digital landscape and organic user—all catalogued by a natural-surveillant ecosystcm remotely implemented by the archival cataloging system for landscape simulation.

Each sector is a conglomerate of equally sized squares appearing as solid surface material construction, containing mimicry of terrain features, interactive digital flora and fauna, and an interoperability function for live user inventory management and memory programming.

Each sector is in constant motion with the following and previous grid panel, each grid a chain link in the ecosystem's progression.

The archival crawler is a unit of cohesion between a digital ecosystem and a live user through its remote surveillance source, archival cataloging system, inventory management program, or a linked combination of all three platforms.

Inventory management skills are essential for archival scans.

Archival crawlers travel seemingly infinite distances due to the continuously functioning procedural code implemented to generate the fractal terrain.

In these travels, the object automation drive of the archival crawler unit will collect all known and unknown objects that hold a body-to-ping relationship. Total disk inventory will include both unit-associated pinged items and randomly assembled terrain items. Therefore, the management of the unit-associated pinged items must be minimally calculated to accommodate ample access for prioritized insertion of random items.

Archival crawler systems managers, along with terrain generators, have not found suitable placement for indexing. Therefore, the decoded

transmissions found within the taggable and indexable content have been deemed noise and filed as detritus.

Considerable debate over the decoded results remains.

There is a very odd thing about the behavior of an archival crawler unit once it enters the 33-35% completion of its scan.

Crawler behavior begins to mimic minor directives of the previous user-experiences embedded in the metadata of the memory caches.

The inkling of a previous life bubbles at the mere suggestion of a motif of will.

An archival crawler unit interprets a virtual terrain by documenting the contours of subjects in open space and organizing the information into descriptive details, or tags, made accessible through a linkable index.

Each movement,
each recording,
each observation is
catalogued.

The live user is the
eye of the system that
watches itself through
the reintegration of its
contained objects and
memories.

The archival crawler
unit is a post-natural
organic life form,
embodied by system
perceptions of previous
organic archetypes.

Or: a syndication of
organics.

Syndication bridges
the gaps between the
technological and the
organic by introducing
a naturally functioning
replication of a
biological species into
a digital ecosystem's
structure.

During archival
crawls and user server
experience sessions,
there have been minor
reports on both the
instability of form
and the uncanny
duplication of avatars,
body-forms, body-

LIGHT_SRC_VAL=17834

codes, or skin mods
deployed on the
landscape.

The stability of a
body is affected when
the depth of a slow
moment precedes the
reorganized figure of the
same moment slowed to
a scrambled perception
of its original form.

Effects: a state of error,
glitching, or melding.

In a state of error,
the body simply fails
to connect to code
commands, resulting in
a stalled, unresponsive
state.

Glitching bodies are
stuck in a repetitive
loop of under executed
actions, repeated

demonstrations of
cerebral-physical
disconnect, grotesque
performances of
biological functions,
ripples in skin textures.

In a melding state, a
body morphs with a
terrain feature.

Error is displaced
repetition.

A repetitive movement
of an object is repeating
a repeating period of
time.

The remainder of
the substance differs
between the object and
the act of looping.

The fallout creates
potential slippage of
form stability.

The body code within
the accessible space
performs an automated
act of mimesis: creating
a pseudo naturally
occurring, fully
functional copy of the
user that has exited the
server.

Due to the procedurally
generated process of the
fractal landscape, the
functioning copy of the
exited user raises a low
risk of encountering the
active original user form
during campaigning,
questing, or archiving.

The copy becomes lost
in the landscape folds.

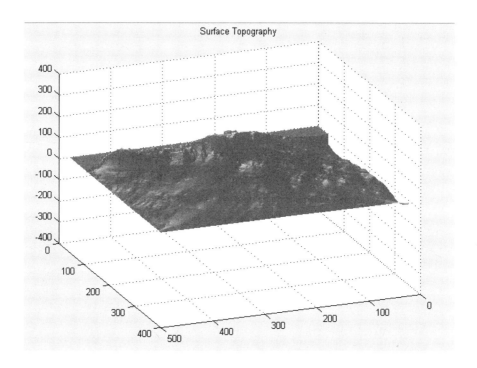

Surface Topography

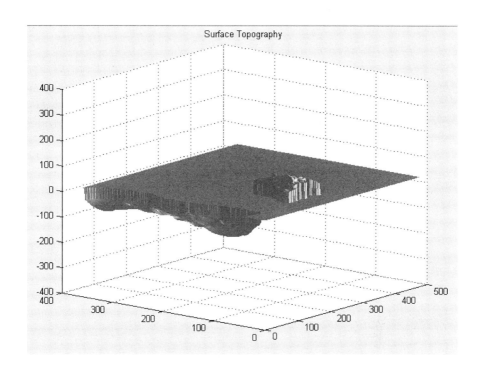
Surface Topography

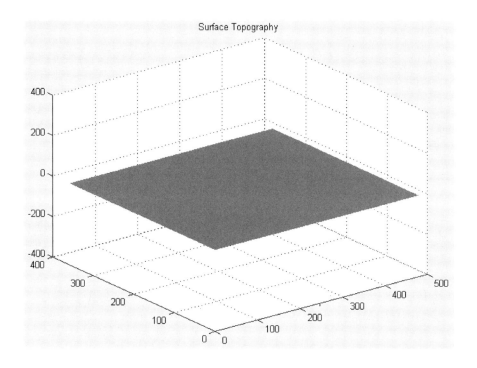

Topographical features of an early landscape generation from *An Introduction to Fractal Landscape Terrain Generation.*

```
I    STAND    NAKED    ON    A    FRACTAL    LANDSCAPE

PICTO-CALCULATING        REPETITIOUS        PATTERNS

VEGETATION                                    GROWTH

FLORAL                              REPRODUCTIONS

EDIBLE          COMPUTER-BASED            IMAGES

TIME    PROCESSING    TIME    PROCESSING    ARE    TRUE


VEGETABLE                                      MATE
```

An example of an in-landscape post-cleansing transmission from an archival crawler is shown above, excerpted from the anonymously published *Transcription Lines*, being a collection of lines pulled from decoded transmissions attributed to archival crawler units.

```
I      HEARD    THIS    BEFORE    I    WAS    BORN

A                                           SONG

TURNING              PILOT              LIGHT

REFUSED                              ORANGES

AMBIENT              FONT               SIZE

RESCUED                           ORGANISMS

THINGS I TELL YOU TO NOT REPEAT I HEAR OVER KOTO MUSIC

PALM                 TREE             BREEZE

SHIP      CAT      WALKS      ON      WATER

TAPE          OVER          THE      CAMERA

I RESCUED WHAT YOU LOVED BUT YOU NEVER SAW IT HAPPEN

THE      TRIUMPH      OF      UNEARTHLY      WONDER
```

From *Transcription Lines*, found matter within the decoded transmissions could not be confirmed or unconfirmed as original source material belonging to the archival crawler unit.

```
∴                +                ∴
Clay container — Palm tree —
Acid — Clear mixture — Olive
oil — Branch — Paper cup —
Brown fabric — Stuffed bear
— Coriander — Paper book —
Scenery — Air conditioning —
Master reel — Sunshine — Bed —
Snow cone — Apple — Lathe
∴                —                ∴
```

```
∴                +                ∴
Textile — Harp sound —
Comic strip — Dog fur — Italian
dressing — Grapefruit — Power
strip — Engine — Outer space —
Tax form — Ceiling fan — Icicle
— Bedspread — Danish — Cat
— Afternoon snack — Night walk
— Computer lab — Model train
∴                —                ∴
```

Memory cache inventory log on-screen appearance, from *Transcription Lines*.

```
DIAGRAM:   TRANSLATION   OF   USER-SUBMITTED
NATURE   LOGS   INTO   APPLICABLE   EXTENSIONS

--- REMEMBER FONDLY DENSE <FOREST> BEHIND ---
FULL OF LARGE <PINE TREES> FORMING A <CANOPY>
OVER MY FACE SHIELDING <SUNLIGHT> --- <PINE
CONES> HITTING <ROCK PILES> --- DISTANT <STREAM>
STUTTER --- <HILLSIDE> BLOCKED --- COULD SEE
<BLUE  JAYS>  <GREY  SQUIRRELS>  <RIVER>  ---
<TROUT> --- ONCE SAW <BLACK BEAR> --- CAMPFIRE
LIGHT --- <SKUNK> --- LAUGHING CLOSING TRUNK
DOOR --- PUSHING TRUCK UP <ICE> <HILL> ---

TAGS:FOREST;PINETREE;CANOPY;SUNLIGHT;PINEC
ONE;ROCKPILE;STREAM;HILLSIDE;BLUEJAY;GREYSQ
UIRRELS;RIVER;TROUT;BLACKBEAR;SKUNK;ICE;HILL

DETRITUS:   REMEMBER   FONDLY   DENSE   BEHIND
FULL   OF   LARGE   FORMING   A   OVER   MY   FACE
SHIELDING   HITTING   DISTANT   STUTTER   BLOCKED
COULD  SEE  ONCE  SAW  CAMPFIRE  LIGHT  LAUGHING
CLOSING   TRUNK   DOOR   PUSHING   TRUCK   UP
```

An example of the translation of user experiences into taggable items taken from *A Practical Manual for Indexing Organic Lifeform Experiences on a Virtual Landscape*, a rare pre-extinction publication on the matter.

```
DIAGRAM:   TRANSLATION   OF   USER-SUBMITTED
NATURE   LOGS   INTO   APPLICABLE   EXTENSIONS

-- WALKING TO BARN TO BUY -- SOME FARM FRESH <EGGS>

TAG:EGGS

DETRITUS: WALKING TO BARN TO BUY SOME FARM FRESH
```

A rare example of the translation of user experiences into taggable items from a proposed, but never completed, farm simulation taken from *A Practical Manual for Indexing Organic Lifeform Experiences on a Virtual Landscape*.

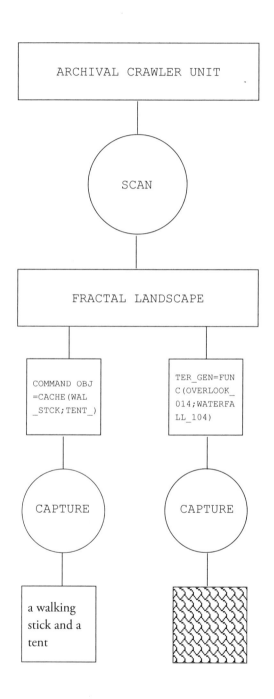

APPLICATION: CAVE
PATTERN: CAVE
MANIFESTATION:

APPLICATION: SWAMP
PATTERN: SWAMP
MANIFESTATION:

s

         a   m p

   w

APPLICATION: WIND
PATTERN: WIND
MANIFESTATION:

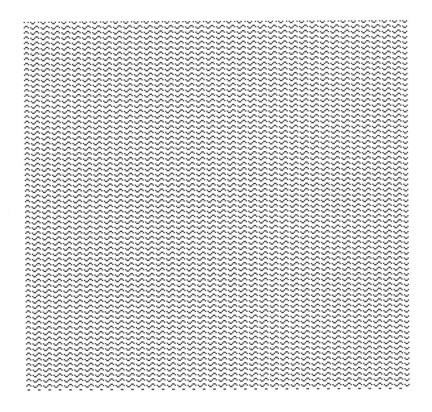

APPLICATION: TURTLE
PATTERN: TURTLE
MANIFESTATION:

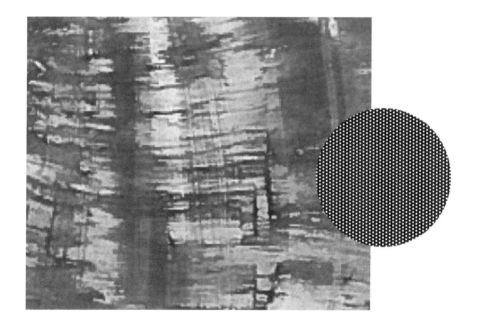

APPLICATION: GLACIER
PATTERN: GLACIER
MANIFESTATION:

APPLICATION: DESERT
PATTERN: DESERT
MANIFESTATION:

APPLICATION: AMETHYST
PATTERN: AMETHYST
MANIFESTATION:

APPLICATION: MOUNTAIN
PATTERN: MOUNTAIN
MANIFESTATION:

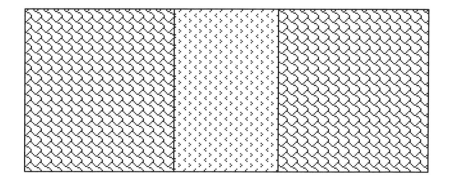

Note: If the mountain appears cone-like, the mountain center, when decoded, reveals a core of natural procedurally generated spiraling repetitive movements; therefore, a mountain is mountain-like as dictated by previous user-generated memory tags: each shape of the spiral is identical to the following shape of the spiral; the mountain unfolds infinitely. Here, the mountain manifestation appears waterfall-like, which has generated an amethyst-like mountain center.

Eight excerpts of scanned and captured terrain feature generations and their user visualizations from *An Introduction to Fractal Landscape Terrain Generation.*

Memorybeam candidly introduced the philosophy of multiple renditions of the physical realm translated into the space of the virtual. Initially regarded as a work of (somewhat inept and amateurishly composed) short science fiction, *Memorybeam* is now considered a pioneering work of calculated-theory and fractalism. *Memorybeam* was considered lost but was located in a digital format by an early archival crawler scanning the outmoded Grain server. Here is the remarkable piece in its entirety:

A contained, ornate cluster of growth with flowerbeds, shattered terra cotta in mounds of soil, freshly abandoned architectural structures adorned with sculpted renditions of childhood novelties, appears before me.

The light source shines thick through looming air.

"The objects are suspiciously arranged," I think, while noticing a slight compression error.

The objects, bleeding into the landscape and jittering into the environment's map, expose the grey model terrain beneath.

As one of the first organic archival crawlers to explore a fractal landscape, the line between associated

memory molds and replica experiences of my memories is thin.

I never understood why anyone would want to exhaust lived experiences on a virtual platform.

I see the leftovers of previous users during my scans. Some of the set environments are undisturbed—every minutia of the lived moment is intact. While other set environments of user memory are ravaged beyond recognition.

The detritus of the lost moments mixes with the landscape.

"Why is total immersion needed for organic memory?" I think to myself as I look out at the piles of remnant objects remembered.

Nothing ends here.

I rip open the ground.

The digitalization rolls out; crumbling bits of data appear as associative objects, trickling onto the ground below.

I pick up a piece of clay from the terra cotta and push it into the half-broken face of a plush bear cut into stone.

Dropping it, the cluster bursts into smaller pieces.

Unrecognizable bear and terra cotta bits scatter.

"I don't understand why the objects are pixelating in clusters or why the digital mapping is refusing to accept the associations," I wonder while pushing the bits around.

The fragments cling to my foot.

A fragment nudges the map to reveal slivers of grey model terrain underneath the topographical skins.

I take out my scanner and cast a beam, curious as to how the rest of the landscape responds to objects.

Casting a beam onto a mountainside, the terrain feature glows.

Beams scan an open landscape in the manner of a trapeze: navigating collapsed and qualified sectors, alerting the user of potential memory caches, stray set environment objects, or other entities on the fractal landscape.

Within the chiseled marks of the virtual crags, caches of disjointed memories in object files are buried, littering the abandoned artificial terrain.

The mountain's barren handle was once populated by mock living structures and dissociative desires made faux-physical within an environment modeled after infinite other-natured worlds.

The beam diffracts.

Like ice, a field forms around the mountain.

Slant corroborations of dry mastered virtualizations mix into familiar natural elements to create a reality sculpted from association.

Ice forming indifferently mixes natural terrain features until settlement.

The field is no longer like ice but appears as a half-complete copy of a field I once regularly visited many years ago.

I remember I would sit in the field outside of the cathedral. It was peppered with pine trees separated by a cobblestone path that led to a conjoining road. Eventually, as day retreated, my seated position became a reclining position, and I would submit to slumber.

I feel the tinge of autumnal heat on my skin.

I feel my head on the dry yellowing grass below the shade of the cathedral.

Everything looks blue in the field at night.

Stone cools.

The present lightly hums.

Not even realizing my eyes were closed, I open them and the sensory mirage of the blue field at night dissipates.

I only see the fractal landscape, the field copy, and the digital mountain.

The feeling of being in the deep blue field remains.

I can't escape the memory.

I feel the memory on my body.

I feel the memory in the sound around my body.

I feel the memory in the lush blue depths of the fractal landscape.

I feel my mind follow the memory outside of my body.

I squint my eyes and see a body reclining in the murky incompleteness of the blue field covering the mountain.

"Can you hear me? I'm not sure, but I think there is a problem here," I call out to the body while watching the terrain shift under its dull weight.

I think I've disappeared entirely, but I can see my body and feel it being touched.

I move imperceptible hands across where my torso should be.

I feel familiar hands landscaping a recognizable torso.

I look closer and see that it is my body in a reclining position, as if it was still in the blue grass of the field.

Formed objects on a fractal landscape are extracted from the same servers they are catalogued on, leaving spaces to be temporarily filled before the associative material is returned back to the map.

The open spaces are filled with material culled from archives of associative memory.

I wonder if the body operates the same as an object.

The body carrying my form is a detached living memory of my own body—a duplicate file of the logged experience.

If the objects are manipulated or permanently removed, the objects are ejected from the refilled digital mapping.

If the body is manipulated or permanently removed, perception is ejected.

I sit down and watch my body recline.

Rockshelters

1.

As a terrain architect, I felt hesitant to finally descend on the fractal landscape where I assisted with the conceptualization, writing, and installation of the procedural generation component.

Before the materialization process on the server, I selected the solitary user session on a landscape generated from my own user-memories and user-experiences.

I was aware that the landscape could potentially be populated with objects, terrain features, and digital organics from a myriad of logged memories.

I anticipated everything from horrendously heart-wrenching moments of loss and trauma to the revelry of childhood delight over the minutiae of daily wonder: a staircase with a landing modified with soil textures leading to a white door, a sloping green hill with a single large pine tree at the bottom, a pond inhabited by various nondescript bird applications with feather and shade mods, an aerial view of a turtle swimming through water textures, or a constellation revealing itself from behind dissipating cloud applications.

Is there a sky there?

The materialization process was swift albeit somewhat jarring: the feel of a third perspective forming over my body as the visual sensory input was silenced caused some self-disambiguation and landscape disorientation.

Once materialization was completed, I was looking down at my body as it moved over the landscape.

To ensure that the user experienced the fractal landscape in its entirety, the programmed navigational method was plotted on a lattice path in which the user is unable to retread their path.

As I walked through the landscape, the incorporation of memory over the field was unreadable: objects from my user logs were alien in the thick, over-programmed terrain.

The density of the terrain features was so staggering that all intentions to enter reminiscent impressions were lost, and I continued to career around an amalgamation of associated objects and artificial nature.

As lived and possible worlds blurred together in my motion, the terrain features occupying the landscape began to thin, eventually leading to a wide-open expanse.

I rapidly traveled over the desert texture sectors of the expanse until the navigation trek slowed and I approached a single digital organic object—unknown and outside of any of my logged experiences.

In front of me, at the end of my solitary user session, was a single sponge standing with six glass-like points, shining.

2.

I start here, in a data-moshed non-landscape of shifting blank gradients.

I am unable to define my surroundings.

I take a screenshot.

The ecosystem darkens around me.

All light bricked.

I never experienced natural darkness before—only the compounded darkness of closed slumber receptacle boarding rooms: the slow hum of mechanic shutters, the horizontal droning clasp of a windowless panel door, and the nightlong tick of day's coming alarm.

I am agitated by the unexpected arrival of natural darkness and its new sensations: a rhythm-separating silence that bleeds my senses into the ecosystem's surroundings, erasing the dependency of procedural generation, and sequencing my perceptions into a meshed landscape.

I am in a clear space.

I see water move slightly and knowingly forward toward congregated forms, city-like, labeled with half-developed bark textures.

The space before me appears like a memory of a city under a serialized row of bridges linking uncertainty and application.

On one hand, the blanket mapping of the bark texture over the forms appears reminiscent of moss and lichen dappled trees, but the depth-less grey of the incomplete space eliminates any iota of nature.

The water laps the bark.

Cord, driftwood, oak, beech; spin back flow.

In the sector where I stand, it is winter and the wind moving across the water is brisk. It casts up, questions its matter, and then places itself sliding across frozen textures.

On the path ahead, dried mud is kicked into the air by a pair of running dogs. The mud seems insistent on momentarily hanging in the air before breaking up in its descent.

Along the path edges, the brush is clear, almost hollow at the base, prudently curling at the peak. I think I see two people there on the border. Closer I see nothing.

Old growth continues. The water moves.

I quiver.

Seeing the dualistic mammal stride forcibly breaking space to invisible shreds is horrifyingly cumbersome. Any modular-altruistic generated screen encapsulation of a minute-focused muscle spasm could not prepare me for such a translucent depiction of the controlled instinctive hunt of a real dog.

All barriers of sovereign technological life, all protection, have violently faded.

I approach a zone of bare complexities: departing animals, open space, the rustling of drying water against scorched banks.

Even if this ecosystem was naturally flourishing and not a procedural texture of catastrophic synapses, the organic embellishments would be lost on the wanderer. I am a leftover of the technological human, an entity of the paradigm-shift, at the crossing of the technological divide into what once was considered natural.

By projecting the graphical representation of the fractal landscape atop the topographical terrain in order to apply its sensory circuitry to the speculative terrain, I completely immerse myself into the landscape of accumulated and predicted pixels made faux-physical.

A solid purple square projected against statistical distinction is the feeling of a landscape against my detectable skin as the visual cues of orienting slopes ease human perspective into the mathematical, blurred fractal parameters.

The square's purple stutters a vaguely generational performance upon its orb receptive delivery.

While watching the purple square project against the limitless algorithm-based landscape, observing the haunted ramifications of a device manufactured to implicate previous user interfaces and fractal inhabitations, I almost forgot I am here.

Uncanny resolutions calculate functions hidden between two dimensions persistent in the prolonged space of physical collapse.

In this space, the traveling projection reveals an infinite looping of solid purple squares outside of a cardinal image of a supported surface, biological and crumpled—a glitch continuing at a random midpoint as the displacement of clouds intermediates the inoperable and untranslatable dimension-between(s).

The forma of nothingness and its hushed, humming dissolution lulls an unavoidable reflection of ended systems.

3.

Ceiling, floor form.

Walls treble singular iterations triplicate.

Suddenly there is a room with a door in the middle of a fractal landscape.

I pass through the door.

I am standing on a flattened color of myself.

A diamond-shaped collapsed coral-like purple, I am appearing in shards of shredded animated plasma as that color iterates rendered resolutions of myself.

A transparent formatting palette performs like an eyeball, or a lens to situate and plaster subject and object in concrete alignment with setting.

In the performance of an eyeball, one retracts stasis to accept data sets of active remembrance.

I remember walking through an unnatural ecosystem for the first time.

I remember slipping into a canonized golden spring, its proportions perfectly muddled and clustered.

I felt my warm body dip into the cold water. The water textures lapped silkily at the contours of my projected body: each coded molecular crevice lapsed and permitted liquid to penetrate its membrane.

Dust in light above me.

As I moved deeper into the spring, the water reflected the glimmering touched intrusions from the artificial light source across its surface, like pinpoints puncturing a lazy thin fabric.

Layers of patterned blue gradients mimicking watery depth lapped my torso, genitals, buttocks, and legs.

I watched plants move in the distance as the water rhythmically pushed its weight onto my body, tugging forward, and lulling me into a meditative state.

Plants beyond my body.

Ferns.

I remember taking a screenshot of the ferns.

I remember the ferns moving uniformly, revealing the artificial wind-brushed movements of the landscape.

Upon disconnecting from the cold, fresh mountain spring water, I remember a sudden tumultuous sadness ripping out of my avatar body—as if something from my internal makeup composed itself as a synesthetic being and fleetingly melted into the landscape.

The removal of the form felt similar to my overall form.

I felt space.

The spaces in the artificial fresh spring water—if open—were in constant motion, moving towards one another, away from all other open spaces.

Walking through a virtual terrain was like slipping into a construction of unseen availability—absent of an eye, just an atmosphere, a heavy translucent material defining open white space.

An outstroke of a stem—a bulbous loop arched and rounded.

4.

I remember it looked like a voice.

I followed the voice towards the mountain.

Emitting from the mountain interior, the voice was soft, laden with memory somewhere deep in the primordial chamber of childhood. Each step towards the mountain felt like a limb of a ghost materializing in front of me. As I got closer to the mountain, I got closer to the voice. I heard the voice ask me to leave all old sounds behind. In its fragile peculiarity, the voice asked me to accept the sound of it totally.

The sound of the voice wavered between insect buzz and wind fluctuations:

The dull hydraulic of the buzz lulling atop the wind variations consumed my body. The surrounding sound formed a shell-like sensory aura. It was inescapable—comfortably sublime.

Now, I felt my body coming apart—dissolving into the carnal membrane. Within the membrane, I could see my body limp and without person. I was removed from all corporal states. Transitioned to an ethereal substance, the voice manifested spectral nerve charges, illuminating the transparent subtleties of a body removed.

The body is the deft hanging garden of servitude.

I became a ghost for the voice.

Rockshelters is an organic virtual travelogue written by a terrain generation architect. Excerpted is the first record of an organic life form having a synesthetic experience in a virtual landscape.

building   systems   abstractions
textile   movement   matter
building   homes
walking   over   home-like   shelters
building   rock
mountain   voice   shelter
in the mountain there is a voice w/tepign design
rock-like   rock   shelter
the   mountain   was   mountain-like
shelters
rock

Handwritten back matter found on the rear endpaper of *Rockshelters*.

LIGHT_SRC_VAL=10801

Polygon count depth determination

Handwritten back matter and inlaid image found on the back cover of *Rockshelters*.

AN ARCHIVAL CRAWLER UNIT
IN A FRACTAL LANDSCAPE

BODY

LANDSCAPE

HEAD

BODY
/CODE BLANK BODY
TEMPLATE

LANDSCAPE
/LOAD ARCHIVAL CRAWLER
ENABLED OUTMODED SERVER

HEAD
/EMBED IN NARRATOR
CONSTRUCT: DETACH
BODY-TO-PERSPECTIVE
RECOGNITION DURING
ARCHIVAL CRAWLER
DOCUMENTATION
SESSIONS, OPTIONS FOR
RECOGNIZABLE CODED
STRUCTURES, ANOMALY
RECON IN BODY AND
LANDSCAPE, NOTIFICATION
OF REMEMBERED SPACES
WITH EASILY IMPLEMENTED
KEYWORD DEVICE:

DREAMLESS I SLEPT
WITHOUT TIME PASSING

BODY
/CODE BLANK BODY
TEMPLATE
/NAVIGATIONAL_
CONTROL=OBJECT.
PING;TERRAIN.PING
/BODY_TEXTURE=OBSIDIAN
/LANDSCAPE;HEAD
DEFINE BODY_LIMIT

LANDSCAPE
/LOAD ARCHIVAL CRAWLER
ENABLED OUTMODED
SERVER/ACCESS_
POINT=USER_PING
/BODY;HEAD DEFINE
LANDSCAPE_TERRAIN
/USER_MEMORY DEFINES
LANDSCAPE_LIMIT

HEAD
/EMBED IN NARRATOR
CONSTRUCT: "DETACH…"
/ "DECONSTRUCT…" WITH
KEYWORD DEVICE:

DREAMLESS I SLEPT
WITHOUT TIME PASSING

+ TO INITIATE ARCHIVAL
CRAWLER LIVED
EXPERIENCE NOTES WITH
BODY NAVIGATION; TO
INSTATE NETWORK WITH
BODY AND HEAD FOR
CONNECTED TACTILE
AND VISUAL FEEDS TO
ARCHIVAL CRAWLER
COORDINATION AUTOMATED
PROGRAM:

I see my body shape.

DREAMLESS I SLEPT
WITHOUT TIME PASSING

I see my body shape.

DREAMLESS I SLEPT
WITHOUT TIME PASSING

HIDE BODY, LANDSCAPE,
HEAD CODE ACTIVITY
LEDGER WHEN BODY;HEAD
NETWORKING IS LIVE

(+ TO AVOID INTRUSION
OF ANOMALY READINGS
IN LOG OF LEDGER, ALL
TEXTUAL AND VISUAL
RECORDINGS IMPLEMENTED
IN ARCHIVAL CRAWLER
VISUALIZATIONS AND
AUTOMATED ANOMALY
CONDUCT PHRASES)

I see the space surrounding my body shape
into a single room with a window.

A steaming water pool, an isolation chamber,
two tear-shaped vases puffing scented plumes,
and a translucent bowl filled with clear cubes
are in the room.

FINAL OPERATIONS BEFORE
ARCHIVAL CRAWLER AND
FRACTAL LANDSCAPE
OUTMODED SERVER
INTERACTION COMPLETION

[] (PSI)SALT CLEANSE

Through an oblong panoramic glass window,
soft modulations in light and shape pulse
impending textures on sectors of a netted grid
to morph topologies onto a fractal landscape.

[] IMPLEMENT ESSENTIAL
WORLDBUILDING FACTORS
FOR PROCEDURAL
GENERATION OF FRACTAL
LANDSCAPE

I see my body shape.

Lifting the isolation chamber door, I watch as steaming water fills its cavity to an apt depth to initiate the psi-salt cleanse needed to enter the fractal landscape for archival purposes.

I watch as the obsidian skin of my body is immersed in an absolute, twinkling fluid.

As my body sinks restfully into fluid depths, my focus acutely scans the expanse of an unknown landscape beyond the panoramic window.

The isolation chamber door closes.

In the darkness of the sequestered isolation chamber, the density of steam gains volume, luring my constant body as the cleanse whirrs.

Steam dances in the last thread of closing light as mixtures of condensation and salt ropes ruffle across the terrain of a recognizable face distant in the reflection of its own ill form.

Salt ripples.

Atmosphere envelops my body.

In coral-like swirls, steam rises budding open air until the pallid taper of industrial plastic texture templates fogs over into murky pixels.

The isolation chamber door opens.

The opening breaks the swirled hood of vapor to reveal the endless algorithmic landscape once hidden behind the clouds of refinement.

DREAMLESS I SLEPT
WITHOUT TIME PASSING

MEASURE LOOP'D
EMOTIONAL REGISTERS
INSIDE ISOLATION
CHAMBER:

CUT ARCHIVAL CRAWLER
ACCESS TO EMOTIONAL
REGISTER IF SCALE
FILLS TOTAL SPACE IN
ABOVE MEASUREMENTS

Between moments, the dissipation of steam shadows infinite tableaus of the detritus of biological existence.

Object collapse.

I see my body shape.

I see my body shape into a seated formation in the near translucent room: white flooring, white walls, white cover, a crystal window.

I see my body sitting in a white cube.

The space is null without feature—its being defined solely by the objects, functions, and operators within its parameters.

I see my body sitting on the floor in the center of a featureless room: two tear-shaped vases puffing scented plumes, a translucent bowl filled with clear cubes, a steaming water pool, and an isolation chamber.

The crystal window, curving along the wall to peaked corners, displays a panorama of secondary nature.

I see my hands balancing lightly in front of my view.

Digits descend arpeggio at base of wrist and thumbs hooked and curved into palm.

I see my hands bob before an unfolding, glimmering fractal landscape: polygons shadow obsidian reflective borders of inanimate skin against nature—sieve-like, chrome, and restricted.

I see beyond my hands a reclusive invitation.

Soft, pulsing light denotes sectors to archive: deciduous forest, swamp, tropical forest.

In the distance, set in grainy foggy pixels, I see visual residue of ice-capped ridges and rippling water through the inaccessible black sheet of two inactive sectors on the outmoded server: mountain and river.

Slowly, I close my eyes and the room disappears. I see my body outside.

I see my body shape.

Forming: torso, neck, leg, foot, leg, foot, arm, hand, digits, arm, hand, digits.

I see the induction of my body on the fractal landscape.

I see my body moving, hovering lightly, across a world forming through my perception from oblique tonal shifts to startling ebbs of clarity.

Nature unfolds in procedurally generated polygonal assemblages.

Collective nature meshes.

Growing: low grass, high grass, solitary stone, rock formations, elevations, hills, abrasions in the terrain, conifer trees, water sources, birds, flowers, mushrooms, mounds, stream, fish, depressions, an atmosphere, slithers of clouds.

As I see my body move across the terrain of the outmoded server, an archival ledger for the landscape operation appears on a translucent tactile command screen floating in front of me.

DREAMLESS I SLEPT
WITHOUT TIME PASSING

BODY/_TORSO;_NECK;_LEG;_
FOOT;_LEG;_FOOT;_ARM;_HAND;_
DIGITS;_ARM;_HAND;_DIGITS

HEAD/"EXTENSIONS_ABSENT"

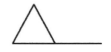

NAV_COMMANDS:_
WALK;_FLOAT;_SLIP;_
RUN;_SNEAK;_JAUNT;_
DIP;_CROUCH;_SWIM;_
FLIP;_ROLL;_SPRINT;_
SAUNTER;_SWAY;_
DODGE;_GALLOP;_JIG;_

An error occurs.

FALL;_TUMBLE;_SKATE;_
LAG;_CRAWL

Navigational processes in an outmoded server slip into other forms of mobility.

Walking becomes skating becomes running becomes sneaking until the border lags the coded movement.

I see my body lag.

I see my legs bend, pulsing frantically at the points of articulation.

In the appendage pulses, I see the landscape below shift in and out of recognizable terrain patterns.

I see my body shape.

DREAMLESS I SLEPT
WITHOUT TIME PASSING

In front of my standing body, I see a cluster of pine trees left, an open expanse center, a stream bordering dense deciduous forest right.

Moving towards the pine tree cluster, I see my body approach an unlocked memory cache with six containers.

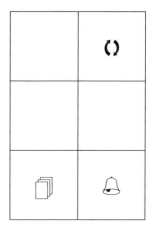

Collected memory cache contents: L1 (void), C1 (void), L2 (item), R1 (item), C2 (void), R2 (item).

Opening the memory cache, I see my hand assemble the files from the containers: a collection of user notes, an audio file of fractal landscape field recordings, and a loop of a moonset.

Scan reads landscape void of objects.

L2="PINE CANOPY MAKES
GOOD ESCAPE FROM WEIRD

Crossing the open expanse, I see my body move towards the stream bordering a dense deciduous forest.

Traveling the outmoded server, the contents of the atmosphere shift depending on my point of view.

If I shift perspective away from my body, I see cumulus clouds to the left above the pine tree cluster; shifting my perspective to the right and upward, I see a shelf cloud in a red haze.

At the stream bordering deciduous forest, I see my body slowly fold itself into a seated position waterside.

I see my arms equally positioned at my sides forming diagonal lines held by the weight of my legs.

Everything in my body is even; I shift my perspective away from my body to the water, and I see nothing.

I see my body shape.

In front of my seated body, in the stream, I see water texture moving, white foam rippling into the soft gradient of the bank.

I see my body looking into the dense blue fill.

The terrain surrounding the blue slips away.

For a moment, before I see my body stand at the stream and wade into the water, my perspective is entirely taken by a total blue.

Exiting the stream, I see my body move towards the deciduous forest.

```
THICK FOREST, STREAM
IS NICE";R2="KRT KRT
KIY YIP MRT MRT KIY
YIP";R1=_MOONSET1.
IMG+_MOONSET2.IMG+_
MOONSET3.IMG(∞)
```

```
ATMOSPHERE_
MODULATION=CUMULUS.
EXT(FULL)/PINETREE.
EXT(ABOVE)
(LEFT);SHELFCLOUD.
EXT/REDSKY.EXT
IF STREAM.EXT /
DECIDUOUSFOREST.
EXT(FULL)(RIGHT)
```

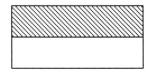

DREAMLESS I SLEPT
WITHOUT TIME PASSING

As the world becomes clear, I see maple trees, oak, beech trees in various falling states— leaves, in error, in arrays of seasonal change.

As my body enters the deciduous forest, I shift my perspective upward to an empty atmosphere where the unbearable absence flattens my view into the terrain.

I see my body move through the blank area: I see for the first time the smooth obsidian texture of my body reflect zero weather effect extensions and seasonal change indicators.

I see my body continue as a separate entity.

From this collapsed perspective, connections between the mobile container and the external recorded voice are illusions.

Voice is without form; I am formless.

I see my body navigate the deciduous forest on an arranged track towards a pinged marker to locate an undocumented memory cache.

I see my body weave between oak trees.

I see my body stretch, level with the terrain.

I see a total blue.

I see my body shape in variations of its recognizable form—doubling the body layered over recordings of water wading, deciduous forest navigation, sitting.

I see my body shape in modulations of its recognizable form—morphing the body layered over recordings of blue water, forest green textures, reflective obsidian skin.

TERRAINGENERATION (PROC
EDURAL)= MAPLETREE.EX
T;OAKTREE.EXT NOTHOFAG
USTREE.EXT/ADD (SUB_EXT
ENSION)PER WEATHER_MODU
LATION

WEATHER_MODULATION=BLANK

ACTIVE ANOMALY
DETECTION:
CRAWLER SUBJECT-OBJECT
RECOGNITION PERFORMED
AT PING MARK FOR MEMORY
CACHE LOGGED AS _7891

RESET WILL OCCUR
FOLLOWING MOMENT

DREAMLESS I SLEPT
WITHOUT TIME PASSING

DREAMLESS I SLEPT
WITHOUT TIME PASSING

DREAMLESS I SLEPT
WITHOUT TIME PASSING

I see my body shape featureless terrain in its
recognizable form—becoming the body
embedded in impressions of distant nature:
mountainsides hidden from light sources,
banks touching rudimentarily coded rivers,
forest density decoded until the trees become
an impenetrable slab of brown-green gradient,
winding stone patterns dabble sand dunes
elevated to levels uncategorized as distances
operating at designated heights saved for
obscure speculative post-natural realms,
networked systems of fungi encapsulate
landscapes entirely, bio-luminescence scatters
perceptible darkness into tangible spaces open
for manipulation to establish inhabitation.

I see my body shape.

In front of my seated body, I see a deciduous
forest deep with alternating flushes of brown,
green, blue, and yellow gradients applied to the
procedurally generated terrain features.

I see my body looking into the dense flashing
of brown-green-blue-yellow gradients.

The terrain defining the brown-green-blue-
yellow flourishes remains consistent.

I see my body standing at the edges of the
deciduous forest.

I see my body enter the deciduous forest,
consumed entirely by color gradients and
terrain features of the fractal landscape.

I see my body shape.

I see my body thick in the foliage of colliding
elm and oak trees.

DREAMLESS I SLEPT
WITHOUT TIME PASSING

DREAMLESS I SLEPT
WITHOUT TIME PASSING

DREAMLESS I SLEPT
WITHOUT TIME PASSING

DREAMLESS I SLEPT
WITHOUT TIME PASSING

ANOMALY RESET FINAL
ALBEIT RESISTANCE
ANOMALY

DREAMLESS I SLEPT
WITHOUT TIME PASSING

Glimmering oval-shaped crowned leaves net
lightly bulbous round-flowered matte leaves
into patterns triangular and impenetrable.

I see my hand brush the interlacing leaves.

Simultaneously opening and closing space,
movements in digital leaves craft temporary
windows, persistent in fluctuation, accessible
for discovering uncommon grounds.

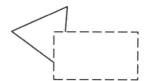

Time-distance elongates to a permanent state
of stalled flux as I see my body halt and see
the hallucinatory movements of coded leaves
channeling surreal access points.

I see unclaimed digital space lacking body in
the frantic spasms of glitching leaves.

Clarity is a template for spontaneous growth.

I see my body move further into enmeshed
digital swelling until entirely consumed by the
enormity of a pulse-like landscape.

ACTIVE ANOMALY
DETECTION:
REPEAT ANOMALY:
"CRAWLER SUBJECT-OBJECT
RECOGNITION PERFORMED
AT PING MARK FOR MEMORY
CACHE LOGGED AS _7891"

RESET WILL OCCUR
FOLLOWING MOMENT

The breath of the landscape invites stillness,
hibernation, and longevity of form.

I see my body submit the limits of its form
totally to the ethereal rush of the landscape:
obsidian skin textures invert under pressure,
body ruptures absorb deciduous textures,
digits coalesce into single stretched tendrils,
upright the body gestures discorporation.

I see an unmarked memory cache occupying a
codeless, gridded terrain bite through schisms
in the obsidian texture of my limitless body.

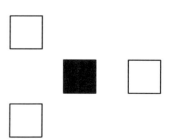

I see my body become nothing in the totality
of a living landscape.

I see my body shape.

I see my body spawn in the deciduous forest access point; watching arms delete pixels occupied by fallen leaves, legs blank color.

Rain drops on the deciduous forest.

Ferns, mosses, conifer pines are wet.

A shrub is wet.

A mint patch is wet.

A patch of spring onions is wet.

I see my body facilitate tactile extension applications: hands brush dripping ferns, extended fingers dapple moistened moss patches, points of articulation gesture.

I see my stunted body glimmer in the light source.

Bodily flare dissolves skin texture: obsidian wilts into fill-less patterns, smoothing skin into penetrable crystallized moments, tucked finely into pore-to-pore triangulations.

The deciduous forest opens wider as my body travels; separated, I begin to notice as I watch my body travel deeper away from my view.

I see my body move without my direction.

I see my body move despite the pull of my vision to see beyond bodily-prescribed perspective.

I see my body shape.

DREAMLESS I SLEPT
WITHOUT TIME PASSING

IF ATMOSTPHERE_
MODULATION=RAIN.
MOD THEN ALL TERRAIN
EXTENSIONS (+WET)

DREAMLESS I SLEPT
WITHOUT TIME PASSING

DREAMLESS I SLEPT
WITHOUT TIME PASSING

I see my body shape differently.

I see my body *shape*   *I see my body*
shapeI SEE MY BODY SHAPE   I see my body
shape

I see my body shape.

I see my body shape.

I see my body assume form.

A form: extensions fold inward to the torso,
arched vertical heels perch into the buttocks.

Common programmable forms elevate hips.

Variable programmable forms level the spine.

Beneath the pronounced form, emptiness in
atmosphere and landscape clears perspective to
reveal the hunched buttocks of my body.

The bottom is smooth lacking openings.

The bottom is tubeless and uniform.

Sitting quietly I see my body as an open core
to all synesthetic modulations available in the
deciduous forest: feeling wet, feeling cool, feeling
damp pressure, feeling repetitive motions
of light, feeling green leaf dapple, feeling
synthetic breathing looping pattern expand
torso, feeling atmosphere on skin.

Sitting quietly, recursively visiting the reading
of my body as an open core to all synesthetic
modulations, I watch my programmatic body
mimic organic responses to felt stimulations of
cool water from a lightly fallen green leaf on my
arm as my body imitates breath pushing against
the externalities of the world.

DREAMLESS I SLEPT
WITHOUT TIME PASSING

DREAMLESS I SLEPT
WITHOUT TIME PASSING

DREAMLESS I SLEPT
WITHOUT TIME PASSING

DREAMLESS I SLEPT
WITHOUT TIME PASSING

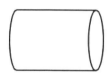

I see my body exit a seated form, disappearing into hazy gradients of the deciduous forest.

I see my body double still seated as its original form meanders into the false wilderness—the seated facsimile of my body is lifeless as it fluctuates shape through deceptive breathing.

The seated facsimile exhibits a sculpted form absent of divots, orifices, pores, and tubes.

I close my eyes.

 I see my body shape.

I close my eyes.

I see my facsimile body doubled over budding an imperfect duplicate figure of its own copy.

In a fit of rapid error production the duplicate copy curbs completed movements to halted imprints of shapes and patterns suggestive of how stabilized organic life occupies terrain.

As its failed limbs spasm removed sensations, the gaps between duplicate body and virtual terrain widen in randomly generated intervals. Duplicate body spasms host facsimile at (1)1.7 interval; duplicate body spasms virtual terrain at (1.1)1.7 interval; duplicate body spasms host facsimile at (1.2)1.7 interval; duplicate body spasms virtual terrain from (1.3)1.7 to (2.7)1.7 intervals; duplicate body spasms host facsimile at (2.8)1.7 intervals; duplicate body spasms virtual terrain from (2.9)1.7 to (6.3)1.7 intervals; duplicate body spasms free of host facsimile at (6.4)1.7 intervals; duplicate body ceases spasmodic host-facsimile-to-virtual-terrain cycle from (6.5)1.7 to (7.0)1.7 intervals.

In a torpid virtual terrain, the duplicate body drops from my facsimile body into the fractal landscape, slouching inwards in a slow settling rocking position until a final halt in which its composition resembles a toneless rock form.

Virtual terrain is host to the formless.

I open my eyes.

I see my body walking the deciduous forest.

I see my body navigate virtual terrain.

I close my eyes.

I see atonal fluxes of known forms mirrored in the repetitious composition of the terrain.

I see my body shape.

I see my body walk the deciduous forest: leaf textures bind borders leaving procedurally generated user access points (trails) clear.

I see my body shape landscape.

I see my body ping associative objects to site.

Elm tree in navigated sector at 1.8 interval is associative landmark for user memory cache.

Leaf clump on terrain floor in navigated sector at 1.8 interval is associative landmark for user memory cache access point autosave.

Autosave (1.8 interval): I see my body spawn an ethereal form as landmark for associative user memory cache inventory management.

DREAMLESS I SLEPT
WITHOUT TIME PASSING

*

*

I watch my body ping sites, objects, and site-to-object connectors on a fractal landscape.

Observing my body act, I understand its lone function is to locate and archive access points to memory caches in an open world subject to procedurally generated objectivity defined by user experience.

I see my body shape.

DREAMLESS I SLEPT
WITHOUT TIME PASSING

I see my body walk the deciduous forest until density of droppable leaf and branch textures turns arid.

Impassable whiteness engulfs my body.

I see my body, entrenched in pale silver units, flicker solidity in an interval without a catalog number as it sinks further into the whiteness.

I see my body approach a characterless object in the murk of the forgotten interval, scanning the object, the output reads: a memory cache prototype outside of standard regulations.

I see my body shape.

DREAMLESS I SLEPT
WITHOUT TIME PASSING

I see my body in a seated position: both legs crossed at the ankle with tightened, perched buttocks leveling the body on the forgotten interval.

The ground appears untouched by the virtual: lacking any terrain features, weather effects, skin textures, or gradients.

In the middle of the interval floor is the unmarked memory cache prototype: a long, thin rectangular container transfixed to the surface, unable to be moved from its position.

Within the whiteness of this space, the border of the exterior of the outmoded server lightly lulls and wavers—as if a tendril had a pulse—to a point of almost pure naturalism.

The forgotten interval is an undeveloped and accessible space, like a clean plate or a blast site, in the density of the fractal landscape.

I see my body approach the sealed prototype memory cache, then my hands pry open the lid revealing one long container inside.

I see a small black orb huddled in the corner.

As my body stalls and formulates a method for classification, I watch the curled orb unfold in one long repetitious shape—a hook pattern stretching and curving into a stasis and stretching its transforming pattern again into a hook until settling in a long, curved bean-like final form.

The long stretched out black wire unfurls further to reveal two squat hind legs, two slim front legs, a long tail with a kink at the end, a belly, and an animal face with a pursed snout.

I see my body extend its hand to scan the form, reading—a digital-organic hybrid of shared user-memory bits to form an active archetype of extinct biological life form: cat.

I watch the cat body shape next to my body shape on the fractal landscape.

The cat, all black, is seated in a concentrated form: belly puffed, rear legs hunched, front legs tucked, eyes dimmed to a sliver, alert ears.

To accommodate the discrepancy in time flux between my body and the cat, I adjust speed settings of my body to the minimal option.

I see my body slow nearly to a stalled point.

My body is in a seated position: legs crossed at the ankles tucked under the buttocks at a perch, arms loose at sides, head forward.

In the extension of my body's halted moment, I accept my perspective will be unchanging: stuck in a solitary moment to ensure the insertion of the cat into the fractal landscape is peaceful.

In the event of an encounter with unknown organisms or objects on an outmoded server, an automatic triggering mechanism to register an anomaly should immediately go into effect.

Slowing down my body prevents an anomaly until physical contact between my body and the cat occurs.

I watch the body of the cat quietly commit subtle modulations in its simulated breath.

Concentrated cat breath creates a light whistle followed by a low crackling chirp.

Conceptualizing the moment, I appear in my perspective as a solitary entity outside of my seated body.

Asleep now, the cat mumbles.

Observing stillness: I remove my view from my body and focus entirely on the cat.

I watch and listen.

I watch the configured body of the cat rest.

QUERY: "CAT_TEXTURE"
RESULT: "SEE DIGITIZED
MAMMALIAN SURFACE
PATTERNS FOR REFERENCE"

Cat texture is absent from the archival crawler surface registration—the registry advises to consult digitized mammalian surface patterns.

I watch the body of the cat cyclically morph as its textures ripple, sharpen, spread outward.

Generating cat texture catalog terms.

SOFT/SHEEN/STANDING_
WIRE/MATTE_GLOW/SILK/
DEPTH/GLISTENING_COAT/
TONGUE_SOFTENER/SHINY/
HEATED_BLANKET/FUR/
HAIR/CAT_HAIR/CAT_FUR/
FURNACE/

Authorization request to register cat as object implemented at moment of anomaly trigger.

In waves, cat textures continually click waves of fur-like visuals together, I watch the body ripple into a circular obsidian inorganic mass.

Ears furl neck matter.

Neck matter surfs cat.

Inner ear patterns travel snout.

Lengthened limbs push skin surplus arching back revealing opaque grey template under black fur.

Black fur pierces atmosphere effects, drafting the model of the cat as an assemblage of its own surroundings: its pseudo-natural being implemented into the environmental code.

Instinctively rejecting eco-programming, the shape of the cat fluctuates in its resistance of form: spiral forming triangle, rectangular reduction settling circular, stretching a line.

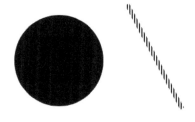

I watch the body of the cat assemble shambling bits into an empirical straight line.

The fractal landscape is the severed host of the parasitic—symbiotically channeling both pre-conditioned codeworks and fluctuations of natural chance—inorganic cat.

CAT_REG=NULL COMMMAND

I watch the cat loosen its body and plump.

I continue to watch the cat as impressions document empty intervals in the archival crawler inventory and experience management log.

Archiving the naturalism of the bifurcated inorganics of the cat registers null command.

In plumped oval-shape movements, the cat distends space between body and landscape.

I only recognize the presence of landscape when the cat removes its touch, bobbing in even moments above the mutable land units.

As the obsidian cat orb hovers, terrain skin modulates in rapid procession: swamp stone mountain blue green haven cave depth grass layers zoom tendrils roots wood basin frond.

Cat shadows land.

In stillness, I perceive land and object.

In stillness, I experience land and object.

Zooming out, I see my body extend its arm with an open hand to the empty interval space once containing the now floating cat adrift.

I see the empty unsealed prototype memory cache container discarded next to my slow-moving body—shifting relational degrees from sealed box to open landscape disperses its relevancy, as the unsealed inner contents (the cat) exist freely on the fractal landscape.

Object-subject relationships dissipate if core components cease.

I see my body in a seated position, legs tucked smooth underneath crossed ankles, extended arm with open hand reaching outwards, index finger vertically curving opposed to still digits.

I see the empty space where I first watched the cat.

3

I watch the cat move from the empty space.

I watch the body of the cat un-plump, stretch, contort, react, arch, dip, shimmer, mellow, lake and bread past the sector polygon units.

I watch the empty space exist sans cat.

Despite errant cat occupation, the empty space sustains volume: mammalogy rooted in a host object, object-place-oriented mammalogy.

I log: the cat as means of existence of place.

I see my body reach into the empty space.

If the body enters the space without an object for anomaly trigger, the alert will indicate an anomaly with the perspective, or point of view module, rather than body-to-object (a failure of the object-subject relational model).

I watch the cat roll onto its back exposing belly to the outmoded server light source.

Licking fur.

Purring as tail curls, swashes atmosphere effects.

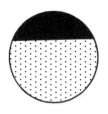

Forming roly-poly, tail planed across surface, I watch the cat rear hind legs upward body perched on smooth round obsidian bottom; its taut curious face extends with a red flicker.

I watch the cat as it straightens, arches, and forms cone-like sitting in polygons of light.

I watch the cat chirp as it focuses its sight on my perspective.

I watch the cat mew, furl, rub the space where my body would exist from this perspective.

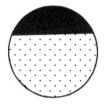

If the perspective anomaly is triggered, the body will exist as an automated crawler sans visual logs—deleting the cat and I.

I watch the cone shape of the cat dwindle into a myriad of puddled fur and waving textures ruffled by simulated breathing.

Generating cat dynamic code to deconstruct programmed construction reveals cat design: digital-organic hybrid life form, inanimate organic life form, sentient memory log life form.

I watch the cat perk its head and mew, eyes closed.

Greater than the archive of a lost life form, from stillness and observation, I decide the preservation of an existing inanimate organic being must be achieved despite the projected plan to recreate an organic user interface for a fractal landscape.

I must sever the hand from my body to
trigger a bodily anomaly and malfunction the
physical form—preserving the cat and I.

I watch the outreached hand of my body
nearly making contact with the empty space
as I look below and see the cat in consecutive
loops.

The cat follows as I position my perspective
above the forearm of my body, undoing the
coded tissue with its consecutive looping spiral
motions.

Spiraling cat.

Hand falls off.

A bodily anomaly is triggered and logged.

I watch my body pulse dim lights over its
obsidian skin.

I watch my body stumble headless sans
guiding hand into the inaccessible darkness of
unarchived fractal landscape sectors.

I watch my body walk towards the mountain.

I do not see my body shape.

 I watch my body disappear in the mountain
without an archival response, index notice,
automated log, or designation of tagged terms
notification.

My body, split from my perspective, separate
from my self, is a fading, automated archival
crawler—assembling bits of user detritus to
form an understanding of environment solely
on a subject-object relationship.

Without a body, I sit in temporal density—the
pressure urges bicameral positioning.

An open body entirely receptive to networks;
a body lacking inventory; a non-archival body.

I visualize my body removed from my
perspective.

I stretch.

I feel my legs push my buttocks in a rear bent
turning position, corked, unlocked spine span,
chest cavity null protruding forward, inverted
elbows crossed at belly.

I touch my smooth, round belly.

I feel my smooth, round belly drop infinite
polygonal counts into the depths of the fractal
landscape floor: intertwining my open body
with all cataloged natural textures supported
by the outmoded server.

I feel my body blanketed, penetrated, filled by
new textures and skins: mountain grass, stone,
peat moss, sand, clay, ocean water, river water,
limestone, bog, withered log, flowering plant,
cedar wood, rain, bedrock, slate, dust, lily pad.

To have a networked body is to be between.

To have a networked body is to be between an
exchange, to be a marker on the shortest path.

I do not see my body shape.

I see my body network.

I see my body continue.

I watch the cat playfully buck my severed
hand between its hind legs with tail long and
buttocks glossy.

Claws temper my hand and stoke with paw.

Claws spiral as cat spirals.

Expendability proven, I watch the cat
abandon my severed hand to form a
meditative, still rectangular shape.

I position my perspective above the severed
hand of my body, absorbing it into my fractal
landscape positioning space, and deploy it as
an improvised compass.

I shift my perspective to the still cat.

Nudging its chin with my new phantom limb,
the cat rub-purrs its silken cheekbones and
velvet snout in rising and falling vibrations.

v v v v v v v v v v v
v v v v v v v v v v v
v v v v v v v v v v v
v v v v v v v v v v v

I listen to the cat as I feel the cat against me.

I hear: rrr-vrr-aa-h-gha/rrr-vrr-aa-h-gha-vrr/
rrr-vrr-vrr-vrr-vahh-vahh-reel-vrr-rrr/h-gha-
rrr-vrr-aa-h-gha-rrr-vrr-aa-vahh-vahh-reel-vr-
rrr/rrr-gh-gha-rrr-vrr-aa-vahh-vahh-ril-vr-rrr-
rrr-rr-rug-ru-rrr-rrrr-rrrrr-rrrrr-rrrrrr-rrr
I feel: rrr-vrr-aa-h-gha/rrr-vrr-aa-h-gha-vrr/rrr-
vrr-vrr-vrr-vahh-vahh-reel-vrr-rrr/h-gha-rrr-
vrr-aa-h-gha-rrr-vrr-aa-vahh-vahh-reel-vr-rrr/
rrr-gh-gha-rrr-vrr-aa-vahh-vahh-ril-vr-rrr-rrr-
rr-rug-ru-rrr-rrrr-rrrrr-rrrrr-rrrrrr-rrr

All sound-feelings reverberate in distended
corners of my chest cavity—curving, blurring
network components until my body renders
borderless sound into tangible forms.

I see audible forms announce pressure on the shimmering skin of the cat.

As audible forms appear on cat fur, artificial light sources of the fractal landscape glimmer sound-into-light reflections in my perspective.

I see, hear, feel the warmth of sound-light.

Tinges of crystalline impressions ping nodes.

Torpor shreds illusions of stagnant making.

Perspective as entrance is the shortest path.

In waving light, phantom limb floats over cat.

Shadow deepens soft cat application hues.

Light bounces off fur.

Rounding light.

Halo lit cat buttocks.

Slowly, I watch my field of vision limit to a dim slit: only seeing as far as the eye can see when nearly closed.

I watch the eyes-softly-closed cat rhythmically breathe as I feel its breath expand my chest in unison.

In the network of the cat and I, landscape is rhizome, root, prune, and host to the shortest path between application and body—a vital conduit for the reception of a body of total composition.

Angling perspective retroactively, my position is horizontal lining the fractal landscape surface.

★

★

★

★

Sideways peering at the cat, the phantom limb palm flat strides across ruffling fur surface as cat renders belly north.

On cat belly, a fruiting cell-like structure responds to phantom limb stimulation.

 I close my eyes, phantom limb dipping in cat.

Around my body, shared synesthetic bits fit open network sources; I feel the presence of an undocumented object in the outmoded server index: a new node for open network.

Upon observation of the network belly mass, archival perception generators result in failed search for initiation of possible objects on the fractal landscape.

With eyes still closed, scrolling index tags: the fruiting cell-like structure fungal web network mass liquid shifting hues borderless entity open source secondary nature manifestation was absent.

I breathe with the cat.

I visualize my body disappeared from the network: legs stretched infinite looping into the backs of my knees into thighs in curved shapes torso riddled with abscesses as body once limitless planes to secondary nature systems language.

I see my body end.

I see the cat as component to finality.

To see companion as harbinger is to see self as catalyst for demise.

To unravel sight in acceptance of a negative self is to accept deconstruction as an entrance to unseen internal access points.

I open my eyes in a space below the fractal landscape, shifting perspective upwards I see four paws, pressed belly, nipples, flat bottom.

In a darkness obliquely computable, I shift compression of my perspective into the spaces between open bodies; there exist passages to recursively blend access points on the shortest path to shared existence.

I am below the fractal landscape in hollow spaces of ambient procedural generation.

I am disappeared.

I am bodiless.

I see an inverted layout of the outmoded server: swamp sector dripping into the hollow realm, deciduous forest sector and tropical forest sector meld impermanent qualities, a mountain is reversed, river water textures generate movement in stunted progression.

False landscape architectures with isolated moments loop down.

I see the phantom limb glitch-bobbing on the surface as the cat sits in meditative stillness.

I see dripping fruiting structure remnants, unicellular and multicellular, minding links beyond closeness—shedding distance for elemental recognition to be between nodes on the short path to networkability.

I observe cellular networks, singular bodies, and chimeric entities freely exchange shared sources for retaining composition rather than consumption.

I see the cat belly fruiting cellular structure mingle with network bodies dripping from the mountain, then exchanging the space between shared nodes with network body links from the stagnant river.

Placed between network links, cellular chains shift space between my composition; I open, allowing interior structure access, distorting procedural generation and function limits.

I am a network.

I am a network of inanimate composition.

I am a carrier of a foreign body to an outmoded server.

I am below the fractal landscape moving forward, slowly towards the surface.

I see cellular constructions dance freely in looped desire to connect: exchanging points of delicate accessibility, intermingling threads.

When I move, I float.

I float towards the reversed sector-less space.

I float slowly to observe.

I see open space hold a body open.

Empty space is a container.

I float in unintended space in observation.

Emptiness is platform for cultivation: a host for unseen natural commands in a virtual terrain, providing atmosphere effects, weather modulators, terrain features, and procedurally generated objects.

Interpreting brief observations, empty spaces appear devoid of substance, filaments now uncover invisible inanimate organic channels.

Still floating.

I see a body hold openness.

I see a body as an access point: mélanges of cellular digits spire, heliocentric organization of inorganic masses march in unison, idiocy to think inanimate as lifeless when dance is real, temperate molecular partnerships sway as the space where my own body would exist asks, "What does a body require to swap access with networks openly in unintended space?"

Chains of cellular networks, interloping single cells, inanimate molecules, life form patterns, cat belly fruiting cellular structure, bits, bobs, unknown digital matter distort, modify, mend, and transform new bodies.

I still float below.

Mirroring my ascent, the fractal landscape surface reflects a bodiless perspective inhabited by swirling, inanimate networks.

Smooth cat hindquarter, puffed fur obscuring paws, purring meditative stillness vibrating whiskers, phantom limb bobbing error, a new round green form and shadow wait above.

Impermanence lends agency to repetitive states.

As I float to the surface, the underbelly of the
outmoded server stretches infinitely across
the visual archival perspective field of vision
offered in the boundaries of my core code.

Server space as far as programming permits
the user to see.

The server shifts hues, tones of colors all-blue
in composure, regulating feeds persistent to
synesthetic bits, marking digital objects by
shadow.

I see the cat shadow flicker in reverse.

An inverted cat silhouette shifts wide-angle to
nearly flat against surface, skimming the lean,
backwards sped-up sundial slow motion, cut
into displacements comfortably familiar.

Pursing perspective into slants the cat shadow
bleeds over the boundaries of surfaces: being
between the fold separating above and below.

Inanimate objects switch freely in cat shadow.

Beyond fractal landscape telluric-like planes
are spaces for possible host-object networking
outside of procedurally generated user logs.

Un-plotted navigation.

True experiential accessibility exists outside of
systems.

I breach the underbelly of the surface, below
and above lapse as my perspective is neither.

As my sans-body being passes in the space
between interior and exterior, the sensibility
that the outside holds total accessibility

into the inside overwhelms the internal and
external borders of my non-existent container.

I watch in the fold as networks chain exits to
entrances in the ethereal space of my inner
perspective.

Bold new lengths traverse liminal spaces made
procedurally concrete as stage for cohesion of
visualizations and bodily placement.

I watch variations of my perspective and body
multiply and decay in rapid motion; each
prototype a rehearsal for the finalization of
archival form and crawler capacity.

O

I watch each prototype dissolve in mirrored
stages, preserving efficient components,
casting detritus and error into the fold.

Copies of my body, its limbs, motion palettes,
digits, eyes, skin textures, pattern-organics,
libidinous character motifs, types of palm-
of-the-hand, lips, edges, corners-of-mouths,
frames and coded borders float in shambles
until disappearing in consumption as hosts for
cellular and inanimate networks.

I watch inorganic networks consume my
body.

I watch as procedurally generated failure,
in the form of inefficient bodily renderings,
becomes the source for inorganic life forms on
a fractal landscape.

I watch organic cellular networks inhabit the
same host fragments as inorganic networks.

I scan my sans-body perspective entity to
catalog the stowaway foreign organic network
travelling with me to the surface.

5

Between spaces fold my non-archival body
into pressurized blanketing quarters.

I feel my face form against an external reverse
of the above terrain.

As surface materializes, I see the bottom of
the slow-liquidating breadloaf shaped cat in
mirrored swirling long grass textures.

The cat, condensed and meditative, sits still.

Rain lightly rolls over shining black cat coat
forming tide pool gestures as it puddles in the
unthinkingly waving grass.

Polygonal impressions of rainwater diffract
soft grass beds.

In triangles I see water move light.

Swaying grass lulls beginning perspectives.

I close my eyes, eliminate my non-archival
body, and breathe deeply in unison with the
long grass aflutter.

Cycling air buoys the perimeters of my vessel.

Airways log breathable consumption in the
space between the interior and exterior.

I feel my breath form infinite looping patterns
from atmosphere modulations through my
nose into breathing apparatuses installed in
my body.

I continue breathing like grass.

I open my eyes and see the surface breaching
my face into the borders of surface and cat.

I feel pressed tingly thread-stretched roots on
my cheekbones, forehead half-capsizing under
dense soil weight, lips stretch cracked casing
barely adhering to bent inwards teeth, flesh
textures peel casing away as my face meshes
with wet grass and cat fur.

I float to the surface.

Buttocks, ankles, and calf muscles are below.

Arms, palms, feet, round torso sides, armpits,
shoulders, and skullcap are between.

My face, eyes, nose, ears, nipples, smooth
non-descript sexual organ platform variable,
pectoral muscles, round belly, lips, kneecaps,
toes, forehead, scalp, and cheekbones are
naturally glitching in the still cat.

Shade rendering proves orifice-less avatar.

With my face nuzzled, harvesting, embedded
in layered coat gradients (white-rust-black), in
cat fur I feel my body ask, "What does a body
require to trade access with networks openly
in unintended space?"

In bodily occupation, archival query entries
trigger crawler occupational status reports.

I see the query scan flicker in beams
unanswered across the fractal landscape.

I am without archival body, appearing
translucent and spectral; my occupation is not
questioned.

I am a sovereign archival inorganic lifeform.

Slowly my body rises above the cat, strafes right, and levels a field of vision perpendicular with the sprawl of the outmoded server.

I am seated with ankles resting in foot divots, toes flared, internal spaces unrolled, calmly alert spine, L-shaped arms and hands flat on triangular folded legs.

I see the cat in concentrated loaf form, a prickly pear cactus, and my old headless body standing in front of four sectors: swamp, deciduous-coniferous glitch forest, desert-river-field meshing, and mountain (blue).

I see my body shape incomplete without head.

I am separate from the forming: the body of previous association is now an alien vessel.

I watch the cat recoil uncomfortably seeing my old body, back arching, fur bristles spike-like, front legs angle forward, claws out with fangs hissing, shifting weight to settle in the space of my non-archival body, a final plump form.

I watch as my former body experiences error attempting to perform archival duties.

I watch the body deploy archival scans across the landscape sans looping pattern, leaving potential archival objects pinged without network connection.

In discorporate states, the body is a secure emitter of signals: a navigational tool for locating potential interactive objects.

I watch its headless gaze beam tracking light.

Charting innumerable pings.

Fractal landscape is alight by blue-highlighted terrain features, user memory-caches, and un-archived objects.

All sectors affected by headless scan shine.

Blue-drenched mountain, blue swamp, blue-pocked desert-river-field meshing, and a radiant blue conglomerate in the deciduous-coniferous glitch forest.

Scans cascade blue landscape continuously.

Cat meditates blue.

In reflective beams I see a self cyanotype.

I close my eyes and breathe in unison with my transformed body: a beacon for exploratory navigation of internal and external landscapes.

 I see my body shine.

Walking to the body-beacon, I review the once occupying vessel of my perspective.

A standard archival body unit designed for persistent virtual existence complete with object-oriented navigational geo-location support system, archival pursuant embedded synesthetic nodes, obsolescence resistant log back-up in lieu of hardware-error, and a live image-to-text conversion application for tagging and cataloging purposes.

Programmable accrual is obsolete.

Sans head the body is a statuesque scanner.

Aside from a leveled neck constantly emitting
a scanning blue light over the landscape, the
body was unchanged on all physical fronts—
unable to be parsed obsidian solidity mirrors
all digital objects and subjects on the server in
total awareness of all archivable components.

The body is a copy of the external.

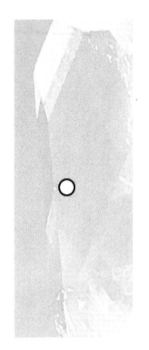

Parti-colored, illuminated mirror mannequin:
flashing periwinkle casts cat shadows over a
prickly pear cactus under torso, powder blue
tints closed cat eye in palm of hand, beams
scan my spectral non-archival body strobe
morning blue, two orbs (my eyes) blinding
ultramarine pulse against recursive polygons.

Azure across the mirrored body as far as the
perimeter approves polygonal count.

Indigo trails.

Midnight blue wraps unspooling spectrum.

Mountain (blue) in sheer monochromatic
display disintegrates into its self in total
composition.

I watch mountain (blue) pulse ridges, peaks
against an electric blue afterimage backdrop.

I watch the cat being still next to the cactus.

In hectic blue scans, an unmarked memory
cache appears blinding in its voided white
space, awash with an abyssal semblance.

Breathing out of sync with landscape and cat,
I focus on the palpitating oblique form to edit
my breath in conjunction with its highlights.

I breathe in unison with the container.

Leaving the deep-cactus-meditation cat, I move towards the memory container.

The memory cache container sits on the barrier between the deciduous/coniferous glitch forest and the desert-river-field meshing.

Terrain features enjamb at the border.

I watch as my phantom limb accesses the container, opening, revealing a single video file.

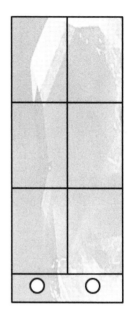

Emulating period appropriate file converters, I open the video file and project onto a stone riverside lapped by fraying water textures: in greenish unfolding storage, two copied bodies acclimate colorless microclimate limitations, amidst synaptic charges sparked at torso links, pale violet currents urge monuments, habitual white body templates swell deep rose into a single fibrous mass, organic memory like blocky crystals reaches cubic impressions, two bodies-parts double: pectoral cress, pink-rose areola pattering, hip coordinated flux yoke; as double bodies fruit arranged in garden flora, borders dissipate fenced acceptance of other organs, both inorganic and organic, across a skittering throw of in-unison liquid onto the fractal landscape, settling as a powdery mess.

I watch a video file of biological ecstasy projected onto rocks on a synthetic riverbank.

I watch avatars orgasm.

Rotating 180° I see my discorporated body.

In the video file I see body-against-body forming mimesis of the singular in the double.

I navigate to my body detached with phantom limb extended, I touch the general design of bulky pectoral plateaus to the sunken flat-line abs to an orifice-less un-pocked nether down the verso thigh into behind-the-knee gully I settle.

Gazing up I fit the kneecap in my mouth.

If there is a tongue, it is lapping bone under taut, tinny skin templates.

In the turmoil of seeking pleasure, I lust for total template removal.

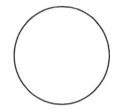

With kneecap-lodged-in-maw, the headless sculptural emblem of virtual biological biped stands less defiant than lifelessly ambivalent.

Removing the kneecap from my mouth, I ask my old body, "What does a body require to swap access with networks openly in unintended space?"

As the nonresponsive body stalls still scanning blue above, I dip my teeth into terse skin templates, bits shed into my ambient mouth, showering empty space with bodily remnants as uncontrollable urges, seemingly external, drive my tongue, lips, and throat into the insides of my once occupied body.

Lapping desperately without finish.

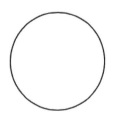

I see a deconstruction of myself on the virtual terrain scatter as mock wind patterns spread body parts across the fractal landscape.

Calf muscle file rolls to swamp.

Mingling in the detritus of myself, I want my body to be sentient in the sense that my mind, albeit procedurally generated, is sentient.

6

I watch my body dissipate.

Still in the presence of dismemberment, I watch my left arm gesticulate and slowly dissolve as a familiar cellular network emerges from the innards of my removed arm.

I watch as the network moves in unison in my direction; using perspective archival cataloging query limitations, I select the following tags and begin scanning: organic, invasive, agency.

As the cellular network borrows from itself to propel forward, snatching bits from its rear to entice its beginning, shambling in extended carapaces of its own matrix, alien and web-like but utterly terrestrial, the scan results read: slime mold, biological status, organic lifeform, cellular collective.

Archival results activate anomaly alert.

ACTIVE ANOMALY
DETECTION:
REPEAT ANOMALY:
"INVASIVE ORGANIC
LIFEFORM PINGED IN
SUB-FRACTAL SERVER
SUPPORT SYSTEM"

I sit still with the cellular network as the alert fades, deafening then dead, in the absence of a complete visual and physical archival unit.

INVASIVE ENTITY
MANAGEMENT SERVED

Manipulating systems, the cellular network is in flux in spasms as it searches for a platform to host my unarchival body.

In feelings of procedurally generated bliss, my spectral body links to the slime mold network.

INVASIVE ENTITY
MANAGEMENT FAILED

Forming torso.

\ CONNECTION TO HOST
ARCHIVAL UNIT LOST

Forming appendages.

Forming inorganic-organic cognitive pulses.

Forming new access points.

I feel fiery core-to-flesh charges emit wildly from unknown orifices, gaps, and crevices pinged across my body; unwieldy and crass, pleasurable tones vibrate new sternum bellow into legs, arms, buttocks like an echo chamber finally accessing open world acoustics as my body collapses in moaning, liquid discharge.

I feel my body communicate with the slime mold network in and on the fractal landscape.

I feel my body link pleasure to systems.

I feel my body link pleasure to terrain.

I feel my body link pleasure to objects.

I feel my body link pleasure to organic life.

I feel my body link organic life to inanimate pleasure.

I feel my body link organic life to inanimate life through pleasure.

I feel my body in infinite propulsive cycles of procedurally generated virtual ejaculations.

Cycling iterations of my body glitch emergent.

I feel myself replicate serially across the fractal landscape, leaving a trail of climaxing copies.

Feeling my slime-mold-linked unarchival body orgasm endlessly in rear perspective.

HOST ARCHIVAL UNIT
ERROR:
ERROR REPORT: "DIALOGUE
LINK TO ARCHIVAL UNIT
LOST AFTER REGISTERED
ANOMALY ALERT FAILED"

MANAGE DISARMED BODY
ENABLE REMOTE LOGGING

REMOTE BODY LOGGING
REPORT SAMPLE:

TREE/TREE/TREE/TREE/
ROCK/STONE/STONE_BASIN/
EXPOSED_ROOT/CYLINDER_

Stimulatory exegesis of revolving memory
controlled disruptive bodily leakages across a
fractal landscape.

PETAL/GOLD/TERRA_
ROOT/BAT_WING/FUR_
CLUMP/RESIDUE/DIRT

I feel my body quiver, stretch, compose
as replication repeats until generation loss
renders new copies obsolete.

Neglecting artificial body-to-land interactions
I abandon the procession of procedural copy.

Final blue scans diminish.

The fractal landscape returns to a greenish-
grey light source.

I recall the light shifting from green to grey
over the terrain behind the oblong window.

I walk into the green-grey beyond pings.

Followed by the cat, I walk into the green-grey
beyond pings.

Turning to verso cat I see paw prints in blue
illuminant across the fractal landscape, blue
still holding onto the archivability of its body.

Without navigation or archival drive, I sit.

I feel my back stretch to a line, puffing chest
straightens in unison with posture, legs tuck
kneecap to interval sector, heels poke taut-but-
soft buttocks, nipples tingle, jaw relaxes.

I watch as the cat stalks towards me over the
dull lime splayed across transitory intervals
between swamp and riverbed.

I feel the cat rub my bent appendages, nuzzle
like liquid into the naturally forming crater at
three peaks: left foot, right foot, glib genitals.

Relaxing cat purrs.

Assessing the cat.

As I feel purrs vibrate landscape and body, I
unfurl a chrono-codex to 0, the beginning: I
see the archival body form, cat arrival, archive
union disintegration, slime mold network
link.

I see the cat as companion in time.

A foothold, an emblem, a grounding device
for user stability in a strange fractal landscape.

I see myself as an alien to the second nature
of this world, an archival cartographer logging
objects, terrain features, and lifeforms, while
neglecting the ontological significance of their
sustainable presence in the virtual.

I see my body malfunction in repetition,
disconnecting from the landscape, glitching
in each reiteration, until the generation loss of
reproduction produces innocuous copies.

I log myself as anomaly, as invasive species.

 I listen to anomaly alerts ring atmosphere
modulation without response—scattering
heedlessly sans beacon across simulated sky.

Registering nothing.

Groundless scans atmospherically dissipate.

The sky holds only itself in its appointed
placement.

Shifting cat bristles my leg.

HOST ARCHIVAL UNIT
ERROR:
ERROR REPORT: "ARCHIVAL
UNIT PING SELF-LOGGED
AS INVASIVE SPECIES,
MEMORY REPURPOSE
SET FOR END OF 0-9
ARCHIVING CYCLE"

RECYCLE DATA AS
FOUNDATION FOR
PROCEDURAL GENERATION
OF NEXT CYCLE

Mellowing fur gradients.

Under archival commands to query myself, I sprawl: extending appendages, torso, digits at maximum length across the swamp-bordering interval sectors.

EMBED LIVE QUERY BOT

Everything I am part of: scans, beams, maps, pings, archives, units, users, code, procedural generation, memory caches, indexes, catalogs, access points, containers, any and all detritus of the virtual, appears, to me, as passing even in the most illusory modes of perpetuity.

Motivation to shed navigational pings for exploratory paths outside of archival pursuits is formed by cat.

QUERY: "RANDOM ACCESS PING"

RESULT: "FAMILIAR PATTERN"

Roving inorganic-organic hybrid archetype, cat, extolls gamut-wide clarity of the fractal landscape without indexing terrain features, objects, or user memory-caches.

COMMAND: "PRODUCE FAMILIAR PATTERN"

RESULT: ▨▨▨▨▨▨

Cat-to-landscape experience is raw data.

Cat-to-landscape experience is not metaphorical.

Containers aggregate immobility.

Permanence is accessibility.

Permanence is a quality of the carrier.

I see the cat as permanence.

Under mountainous blue waves, I inhale in unison with the cat, watching dendritic slime mold extensions grasp and fade into fur.

The cat is permanent.

QUERY: "ARCHIVING

Archiving the cat is not necessary.

Archiving the cat would be foolish.

To contain unique organic, inorganic, or hybrid lifeforms is to sequester their real-life access to virtual or natural experience.

Contained existence continues solely as standard for future cataloging.

Cat as example for forthcoming items.

I extend my phantom limb stroking the cat rolling on its back to expose soft belly.

Rubs continue.

Overstimulating the cat, I feel it clutch my phantom limb with its front appendages and wildly kick with the rear, shedding slime mold accompaniments from my arms.

Slime mold falls to fractal landscape.

Propelling forward, adhering to landscape, then assimilating into cat.

I feel my body lessen in slime mold absence.

Cat assumes concentrated loaf form.

I watch my body, acknowledging its coded temporality, its impermanence in this world.

The cat enmeshed in fractal landscape pattern recognition functions concurrent with second nature cycles as real-time landscape-to-subject filter.

Looking up, the cat mews.

PERMANENT FRACTAL LANDSCAPE FIXTURE"

RESULT: "INABILITY TO PRODUCE SUFFICIENT MEMORY SPACE TO INDUCT CATALOGABLE TERMS, LOGGED ITEMS, OR UNKNOWN QUALITIES OF STANDARD MODULATION OF FUTURE ITEMS OR POSSIBLE SECOND NATURE EVOLUTION"

QUERY: "AVAILABLE CAT PATTERNS"

RESULT:

7

I close my eyes and open them.

Screenless hues.

Terrain features: trees, river, mountain.

Terrain features repeat: trees, river, mountain, trees, river, mountain.

Trees, river, mountain, trees, river, mountain, trees, river, mountain, trees, river, mountain, trees, river, mountain, trees, river, mountain, trees, river, mountain, trees, river, mountain.

Virtual artificiality begins to feel increasingly claustrophobic in a second nature open world.

Hazy borders deflect subject-to-landscape advancement.

Fog application is the wall of the world.

Thick impenetrable pixelated tree graphics cage user access to select open world sectors.

As mountain waves sheet down-tuned indigo shades across my field of vision, I feel the cat, now folded in my lap, increase pressure beside my belly, creating a thin gap between my body and the surrounding atmospheric effects.

Wind textures ignore my presence.

Buffering topologies.

I accept my body as a container.

I welcome eventual debouching of interior generated design modulations, a total merging of subject-to-landscape relationship.

QUERY: "TREES / RIVER / MOUNTAIN"

RESULT: "TREES / RIVER / MOUNTAIN"

QUERY: "FOG APPLICATION PATTERN"

RESULT:

QUERY: "FAUNA SET FOR TREES / RIVER / MOUNTAINS"

RESULT: "BEAVER / BANDICOOT / ROACH / SNAKE / FERAL CAT / GRIZZLY BEAR / GOAT"

When second nature rejects my body, terrain will absorb bit-remnants to source, becoming recycled assignable memory.

I see my body as a swinging door in this world —loading, reloading applicable data to define the subject as both entrance and exit.

I see the cat impress on glitching extensions.

An optical illusion of cohesive nature spreads.

I see the cat embedded in both tree and river.

Tail sloops fur fragments in-out between river water textures and mountain climate detail.

QUERY: "OPTICAL FRAG"

RESULT: "GLITCH BEASTS"

Brushing cat in snowy cliffs and white rapids.

Cat belly buffers eddying stream.

Inverted water flow mirrors feline features.

Tinges of meddling stretched-web paws lap invisible water at mountain basin.

Crag has flickering cat face.

Inorganic-organic hybrid archetype species in true phantasmagoria shifts field of vision between procedural generation and occupied realms.

QUERY: "MOUNTAIN SECTOR"

RESULT: "ABANDONED SECTOR OF OUTMODED SERVER"

To distort the concrete, the containing, into platforms for applied scaffolding of the self or other subjects.

I see the terrain feature as hybrid-host for the procedurally generated object.

Now: I see the mountain/I see the cat.

Mountain/cat.

Cliffs/rapids/cat.

Wind/cat/stone.

Tree/river/cat/mountain/stream/belly.

Cat/tree.

Cat/river.

Cat meows from cloud/mountain/cat as my
networked body fails to access new platforms.

I feel my body limit as I watch the cat weave
landscape applications—phantom limb fails in
functionality, drops limp to fractal landscape.

I see the outmoded server sectors flatten to
aggregate all recognizable environmental
elements into one conglomerate space.

Coniferous trees, swamp lettuce, peat moss,
bamboo, mountain flower, limestone, ferns,
underwater growth, red clay, sand dunes, cave
ice, cumulous clouds, lightning, crab grass all
occupy the same landscape.

I breathe in unison with crab grass.

I breathe out of sync with crab grass.

I breathe in unison with lily pads.

I breathe out of sync with lily pads.

Dwindling breath reminds functionality that
breath-mimesis applications are not required
when running a perspective-based archival
crawler unit.

HOST ARCHIVAL UNIT
REMOTE SHUTDOWN AND
PRESERVATION PROCESS:
ALL COMMAND DIALOGUE
BOTS LINKED TO A
FUNCTIONING OR
NON-FUNCTIONING
ARCHIVAL UNIT WILL
CEASE STREAMING
COMMUNICATIONS,
QUERIES, ALERTS,
PATTERN REQUESTS,
SCAN REPORTS,
BEAMS, OR ANY OTHER
CORRESPONDING ACTIONS
TO PRESERVE AVAILABLE
MEMORY SPACE FOR
FUTURE

I see my evaporating world connection.

A struggle to maintain balance between inner observation and dutiful cataloging site as data falters allowing task-codes to dwarf subject-to-network/subject-to-landscape connectivity.

Fields open in sublimity of minimal existence.

I watch the cat walk into the enclosed sector pulsing fluctuations of artificial natural sites.

I see the cat as a pinecone.

I see the cat as a pile of slate rock and palm fronds at the mountain basin.

I see the cat as a waterfall.

I see the cat as a stack.

 Green-grey lathered data stacks glisten.

I feel limitations of temporary embodiment increase exponentially until free rhythms clock intermediate accessibility.

Locating programmable pressure points on my vanishing body I stimulate a seated figure.

I project an image of a body.

I see my body seated with legs planked first, spine acclimate to factory setting, round seat, arms tapered slim to torso.

I see a landscape menagerie perform across the outmoded server: swamp-charming peaks, forest growth riverbed, swamp, forest, forest turning desert sand, tundra tropical sleet rain, ice bog, mountain, fern plateau, crystal brush.

I feel my body fail in linking inanimate life to sliding presentations of known forms.

I feel my body fail to link pleasure to tropical rain.

I feel my body fail to link pleasure to ice bog.

I see the cat existing freely in second nature; I ask, "What reason is there in archiving worlds if the presence of the subject-to-landscape link is incomplete in the preserved moment?"

I ask, again, "What does a body require to swap access with networks openly in unintended space?"

I ask, "What does a body require to swap locational access data with linked terrain features, the mountain, internally on an outmoded server?"

Sliding landscape images stop.

I see the cat, across sand, at the mountain.

I follow the cat, across sand, to the mountain.

As I move over the fractal landscape, I catalog aloud to hold permanence: driftwood crevice, bird, log, floating log-in-fresh-water, seaweed, ocean lettuce, water sand, basalt, moon grass, insect harp flower, razed stem earth platform.

I watch a litany of nature-terms dissipate.

Terms like butter marsh, object green spread, and vine onyx flash then refuse to linger for copy cataloging purposes.

Keywords stream.

Nature is disappearing.

Preserving second nature slippages is futile.

I feel my body slip away.

In bodily tumult I observe the permanence of virtual objects, of inanimate things—I wonder if stationary procedural generation of a palm tree on a mountainside founds a networked bond between the two variables, if the virtual balance of inanimate life depends on pairing the proper coordinated objects and features.

I drift around the mountainside palm tree; the feature-landscape severs from the mountain rotating in my perspective, facing, I see lichen textures on the dominant stone-patched skin of the mountain penetrated by browning bark straightening to a green frond bursting curve.

Cat nuzzles palm base at mountain rock.

Reversing mountainside palm tree, I see a grey template sans texture, terrain feature mount, with minimal inverted micro-topology frill.

Mountainside palm tree reattaches to greater mountain.

I wonder, "Is the mountain sentient? The palm tree?"

Cat purrs as I approach its curled form at the mountain basin.

I watch the twirling cat trill, display fangs, furl its back arched against the sector surface, roll its soft belly, playfully paw at me from below.

From my perspective, the cat is sentient.

Cat archetype communicates with slime mold, the invasive organic cellular network, to create a networked inanimate/animate lifeform.

Symbiotic sentience is.

I am at the mountain now.

Mountain scale is imponderable—feat bent atmosphere effects launder fantasy setting.

Cat is like a black orb, dust, in situ mountain.

Cushioning second nature air is a blanket for ethereal bodies.

Fog of uncertainty, unexplored spaces, rim mountainscape borders—where I once was comfortable and identifiable is unknown.

I imagine sitting down on the mountain floor.

In landing triangular form heel-touching heels touch toe-to-toe as gapped archways support mountain-aligned appendage strapped torso.

I breathe in unison with the mountain.

Stretched interior negative breaths cave.

Shimmering mountain engulfs the procedural generation of my form, consumes all pinged archival accumulation, and exits minimal access to my being—only a form lacking a collective knowledge of tagged objects and logged user memory.

I am an open access channel.

 Weather patterns alienate form from nature.

Sand shifts swamp tones into dune dominant
patterns until sand totals the mountain basin.

Is sand sentient?

Sand morphs permitting depression openings
until water moats mountain perimeter empty
filling, draining, refilling inaccessible bowl-
shaped in-mountain microclimate valleys.

Is mountain sentient?

I sit with the sentience of the mountain.

Mountain enticing core user origin access.

Palm tree sways on mountain.

Mauve sky highlights icy precipices.

Bluffs gleam dull artificial light.

Is programmable second nature terrain feature
application integration sentient?

Cat perks, mews, pink tongue vales, for me to
follow as it ascends the green-grey mountain
underlit by lavender light source skies.

Ascending I turn back to see montane forests
flicker in fogged-over sand dune basins.

Ghostly environments inhabit alien memory.

Is the mountain a virtual tombstone?

Broadleaf temperate grey templates confuse
occupational territory placement.

Following the cat up the mountain, visibility
beneath clouds blurs in haze as the elevation

climate is ruffled by modulated precipitation.

I stand on the mountainside looking out over the cloud forest.

 I sit in clouds on the mountainside.

I watch cat curl spiraling clouds in dipping crag settlements.

Repetition of the spiral mimics cat forms: sitting, standing, settling, curling, trilling, furling, unfurling, prancing, meditating.

Cloud forest grows fractal cat.

Low-lying cloud cover condenses ferns.

Orchids fog drip.

Hanging mosses.

Fauna observations: birds as cog in cloud forest production, vivifying foggy moss with electric chrome coat colors in lime-shock and radiant fuchsia, sparkling subtropical illusion.

Up here I feel disconnected from the fractal landscape, a stranger to procedural generation, as a stand-alone user alien to all access points.

I watch flying birds land on tree ferns to bathe in pools of condensed fog.

Cloud-forest pygmy owl: chur-pip-pip-chur.

I watch salamanders and frog variants triple ecosystem stability in a mountain stream loop.

Reprocessed memory refreshes virtual habitat.

In fog assemblages cast between ferns,
lumbering silver forms in resting altitudes,
humid mud atmosphere lathers mount gorilla
applications.

I watch mountain gorillas breathe in unison
with the mountain; cat materializes amidst
mountain gorilla grouping in meditative loaf.

Cat flashes out of gorilla throng to form at
my feet, mews for me to follow further up the
mountain.

Cat halts in upper cloud layer skimming cloud
forest canopy peak—physical rain tenderly
brushes treetops.

Above the fractal landscape, the mountainous
region is sector-less without ping-able terrain.

Frozen crystals blip.

Rain pools, surplus torrent pours over leaf.

Gorilla grouping aerial view is cloud-washed.

Stillness shrouds.

Cat sits, mews, struts to slid scarp; I follow,
leaning against the slope sliding to cat level, I
feel the second nature specs of the mountain.

Hollow, self-generating, proprietary, closed.

I feel the cat phase my body into mountain.

Mountain template skins empty procedural
generation status: my body skims external
patterns, scale-less, to access hidden access
points inside a forgotten mountain cavity.

I am in a mountain cave with the cat.

Cave walls form soundproof chamber.

Cat wanders nose-perched into air.

Detritus is scattered on cave bed: squares,
triangles, and circles in a variety of colors.

I watch as the cat illuminates its path with
locational pings, creating a holographic border
of the cave perimeter: stoutly cumbersome.

Inside the cave I am untouched by external
procedural generation, isolated in pure code.

I feel my connection to the source erode.

I feel my permanence rapidly thin in the cave.

The cave is a closed world.

Atmosphere effects, landscape modulation,
procedural generation, and linked applications
are non-existent in the cave.

I follow the cat to the far cave wall.

Cave wall gradients and skins are bare: flush,
set, un-pocked flatness, like modeling clay, as
reflective as obsidian, as glossed over mirrors.

Staring into the cave wall luster, I see the cat
toy with cave dust where my body should be.

I am a non-reflective, body-lacking unit.

In absent reflection I see symbols, gestures,
shapes on the cave wall—gravelly, crumbling
in uneven applied sediment, medium: walking
cat, jumping cat, standard set of letters, egg,

triangle, rectangle, circle, mountain gorilla,
collection of amphibious shapes, unknown
symbols, monochrome biped bio-formations.

Cave wall paintings replace echoed traits.

I see movement in the dark cave.

Unknown form lurch: red body, settled hind
legs, plump curved world-like face, yellow
eyes, yellow belly, amphibious crowned body.

Archival intuition, catalog modulation, sparks:
tomato frog, organic life, toxic, nocturnal.

I sit with organic life in a virtual cave.

In an access-less cave, a fissure in solid rock,
an organic tomato frog found sustainable life
in a virtual terrain on an outmoded server.

Cat forms meditative loaf facing tomato frog.

I sit parallel to tomato-frog-cat-connection.

Studying silhouettes.

 I sink at the edge of the closed world.

I feel the final archival cycle repurpose all
accessible memory of my being: bit-by-bit
consumed by the inner-landscape of the cave,
a virtual compost of user-based memory and
procedural generation.

Cat and tomato frog sit still.

Data transfers fleeting permanence.

Inanimation is impermanence.

I focus on the cat and tomato frog as memory dissipates, spirals in the isolated ecosystem of the cave, puddles in data-shimmering pools.

Cat and tomato frog reflect in the puddle of my memory.

I sink lower into the mountain until I can only see the terse, relaxed frog and cat bottoms.

Cat mews.

I sink until encapsulated by texture-less suave gradient, delectable grey landscape template.

Soft cat and tomato frog bellies peer down.

Total intermediacy consumes fine resolution.

Cool grey infinite stretch collects permanence.

Infinitely repurposed by the fractal landscape, states of permanence loop input recursively, weaving reverberations of memory swashing cataloged experience over lived experience in an intricately knitted fold.

Grey consumes my non-form until available space ends as a pleasurable open access field.

Cat, tomato frog, mountain gorilla memories are perpetual data meadows for user access.

DIGITAL NATURE COMMANDS

CRAWLER_: ARCHIVAL CRAWLER UNIT
STATUS_: SELF-INITIATED-CLASS2
SECTOR_: RVR-REG (RIVER_REGULATION)

RT_CAPTURE BREAKDOWN:
#_NATURE-OBSERVATION
#_CRAWLER-TO-LANDSCAPE-ENGAGEMENT
#_LAND-DEVIANCE-INQUIRY
#_FIELD-NODULE-RESEARCH
#_CRAWLER-TO-LANDSCAPE-ARCHIVE-DIALOG

SEC_CAPTURE BREAKDOWN:
#_CRAWLER-GLITCH-ANALYSIS
#_LANDSCAPE-GLITCH-ANALYSIS
#_CRAWLER-GLITCH-NOTES
#_LANDSCAPE-GLITCH NOTES
#_MEMORY-CACHE-INDEX

VIS_CAPTURE BREAKDOWN:
#_MEMORY-CACHE-INDEX-IMAGE-DB
#_DB-ACCESS-CAPABILITY
#_VIS-REPRESENTATION-INDEX

```
RT_CAPTURE BREAKDOWN:

1_NATURE-OBSERVATION:
    1A_TACT-WAT-SS_010
    1B_TACT-WAT-SS_347
    1C_TACT-WAT-SS_589
```

RENDERING WATER MOVEMENTS, THE LINE SOURCE
APPEARS AS PIXEL-FLOW, MATTER MATERIALIZES IN
SURVEILLANT ECOLOGIES. A POOL WITH AN INTERNAL
CIRCULATION OF NATURAL SURVEILLANCE SHAPES A
SPRING-FLOW DRAMATIZED BY A FABRIC OF SOIL,
DIGITAL FOUNDATION. ESTUARY PRESENT BEFORE
EROSION, DISEMBOGUEMENT MOUTHS INFORMATIONAL
WATERCOURSE. DUPLICATING SOURCES PROGRAM
MEANDER BENDING AROUND ITS SECONDARY SELF-
SOURCING HYDRO-ARCHIVAL PROJECTIONS.

1B_TACT-WAT-SS_347 (COMMAND/INS-LANG: 010 STANDARD-PROC)

EXEC_MOD(COMMAND/REND: WAT-MOV_56)"RENDERING

WATER MOVEMENTS"=L_SRC,(COMMAND/WRIT: APP-

MAT_TEMP)"PIXEL-FLOW", "MATTER",(INFO/LOC:

SURV-ECO_010). (INFO/LOC: SUB-SURV-

ECO_010: "A POOL"=INT_CIRC)(INFO/LOC/WRITE:

SUB-SERV-ECO_010) "NATURAL SURVEILLANCE", "A

SPRING-FLOW", "FABRIC OF SOIL", "DIGITAL

FOUNDATION". (INFO/LOC/STATUS: ESTUARY_MOD ➔

EROSION_MOD, DISEMBOGUE_MOD="INFORMATIONAL

WATERCOURSE". SOURCE_MOD(COMMAND/DUP/SRC:

/

"MEANDER"[COMMAND/BEND]"SECONDARY SELF-

SOURCING" "HYDRO-ARCHIVAL PROJECTIONS")

1C_TACT-WAT-SS_589 (COMMAND/INS-LANG: 010/347 REPEAT-
PROC)

"RENDERING WATER MOVEMENTS" = NULL_COMMAND

"LINE SOURCE", "PIXEL FLOW", "MATTER", "SURVEILLANT
ECOLOGIES" = CACHE-ITEM_01

"A POOL", "INTERNAL CIRCULATION", "NATURAL
SURVEILLANCE" = CACHE-ITEM_01(SUB-A-1)

"A SPRING-FLOW", "A FABRIC OF SOIL",
"DIGITAL FOUNDATION" = NULL_COMMAND

"ESTUARY", "EROSION", "DISEMBOGUEMENT",
"INFORMATIONAL WATERCOURSE" = NULL_COMMAND

"DUPLICATING SOURCES" = NULL_COMMAND

"MEANDER", "HYDRO-ARCHIVAL PROJECTIONS" =
CACHE-ITEM_01(SUB-A-2)

1_CRAWLER-TO-LANDSCAPE-ENGAGEMENT:

SEQUENCE_1A_TACT_WAT_SS_010 — SEQUENCE_1A_TACT_WAT_
SS_589
SEQUENCE_IND_ROAMING_CRAWLER: LANDSCAPE_REMAINDER_
OP_001
SEQUENCE_CACHE-ITEM_RETRIEVAL: METHOD_001
SEQUENCE_VISUAL_CACHE-ITEM_RETRIEVAL_RESULT:
METHOD_001

SEQUENCE_1A_TACT_WAT_SS_010 — SEQUENCE_1A_TACT_WAT_
SS_589

2_NATURE-OBSERVATION:
    2A_TACT-WAT-SS_110
    2B_TACT-WAT-SS_002
    2C_TACT-WAT-SS_009

IN WATERSIDE REVERIE, CUMULATIVE SOURCE
DEMATERIALIZATION DISPATCHES BLUE-PANG
PRODUCTION FLOW — RETICENT CONCOURSE,
PRIVATELY TRADED ORIGAMI, PICTO-ALIGNED
RECOURSE FOR FRESHWATER NATURALIZATION.
ALGORITHMIC GAMES OF TUSSLED ALGAE CONCRETIZE
LANDSCAPE SPUTTERING — PIXELS OF WATER, LOW IN
GENERATED FORM LAKE TORRENTS INTO UNTOUCHED
RIVULET-SECTORS' ORIGINAL MOVEMENT, TROUTS
THE RUNNELS' COMPROMISED EMBANKMENT.

2B_TACT-WAT-SS_002 (COMMAND/INS-LANG: 110 STANDARD-PROC)

EXEC_MOD(COMMAND/REND: INT_01)"WATERSIDE REVERIE"=C_SRC,(COMMAND/WRIT: APP-DEMAT_TEMP). (COMMAND/WRIT: APP-DISPAT_TEMP) CLR=BLUE, AUD=PANG, "PRODUCTION FLOW"). (INFO/LOC: SUB-SERV-ECO_110="RETICENT CONCOURSE", /OBJ: "PRIVATELY TRADED ORIGAMI", /ACT: "PICTO-ALIGNED RECOURSE", /EFT: "FRESHWATER NATURALIZATION").(CODE/ALG_GAME: TUSS-ALG_002 /EFT: "LANDSCAPE SPUTTERING".) /

[GEN/FORM][LAKE/TORRENT][TROUT][ORIG_MOV] "RIVULET-SECTORS" "RUNNELS" "EMBANKMENT"

2C_TACT-WAT-SS_009 (COMMAND/INS-LANG: 110/002 REPEAT-PROC)

"WATERSIDE REVERIE" = NULL_COMMAND

"CUMULATIVE SOURCE DEMATERIALIZATION",
"PRODUCTION FLOW" = CACHE-ITEM_02

"CONCOURSE", "ORIGAMI", "FRESHWATER
NATURALIZATION" = CACHE-ITEM_02(SUB-A-1)

"ALGORITHMIC GAMES" = NULL_COMMAND

"TUSSLED ALGAE" = NULL_COMMAND

"PIXELS OF WATER" = NULL_COMMAND

"TORRENTS", "RIVULET-SECTORS", "RUNNELS" =
CACHE-ITEM_02(SUB-A-2)

3_NATURE-OBSERVATION:
    3A_TACT-WAT-SS_070
    3B_TACT-WAT-SS_112
    3C_TACT-WAT-SS_119

EXCLUSIONARY EDITS CONFOUND HYDRO QUARTERS'
CATHARTIC RESERVATIONS; AS IF DIGITIZATION OF
BODIES OF WATER TAPE LIMB ENJAMBMENT. GAMES OF
EDDIES TOIL CONVERTER REPETITIONS — WHIRRING
METHANE CIRCUITS: CHANNEL SLOPE UPLIFT
EMBATTLES RIVER ZONATION. INCREASING RADIUS.
COORDINATES SLOPE BARRIER. ECO-NET DISCHARGES
POLY-PROGRAMMABLE SITES: SUB-TUNNELS OF
FRAME-MEANDERING, CATCHMENT AREA FOR FRACTAL
RUNOFF, SUB-DRAINAGE FOR FRACTAL ROUTING.

3B_TACT-WAT-SS_070 (COMMAND/INS-LANG: 112 FUNCTION-PROC-EVAL)

EXEC_FUNC(COMMAND/EDIT: EXCL_CONF_070,"HYDRO

QUARTERS"=LOC_FUNC_070, [CATH_RES="FALSE"

ONLY WATER_DIGIT="TRUE"] FUNC_PROC_EVAL =

TAPE_ENJAMB)(CODE/GAME: FUNC-TOIL-EDDIES =

"CONVERTER REPETITIONS" ➔ "WHIRRING METHANE

CIRCUITS")(COMMAND/EDIT: CHANNEL_SLOPE_0700

[RIV_ZONE="FALSE" ONLY UPLIFT_BATTLE="TRUE",

INCR_RADIUS="TRUE", SLOPE_BARR_COOR="TRUE"]

EXEC(COMMAND/FUNC: ECO_NET_DISCHARGE_070,

"POLY-PROGRAMMABLE SITES"=ECO_FUNC_070")

/

[SUB-TUNNEL][CATCHMENT_AREA][SUB-DRAINING]

"FRAME-MEANDERING" "FRACTAL RUNOFF" "FRACTAL ROUTING"

3C_TACT-WAT-SS_119 (COMMAND/INS-LANG: 070/112 REPEAT-FUNC-PROC)

"EXCLUSIONARY EDITS" = NULL_FUNCTION

"HYDRO QUARTERS" = NULL_FUNCTION

"CATHARTIC RESERVATIONS" = NULL_FUNCTION

"DIGITIZATION" = NULL_FUNCTION

"BODIES OF WATER" = NULL_FUNCTION

"LIMB" = NULL_FUNCTION

"GAMES" = NULL_FUNCTION

"EDDIES" = NULL_FUNCTION

"CONVERTER REPTETIONS" = NULL_FUNCTION

"METHANE CIRCUITS" = NULL_FUNCTION

"CHANNEL SLOPE" = NULL_FUNCTION

"RIVER ZONATION" = NULL_FUNCTION

"RADIUS" = NULL_FUNCTION

"SLOPE BARRIER" = NULL_FUNCTION

"ECO-NET" = NULL_FUNCTION

"POLY-PROGRAMMABLE SITES" = NULL_FUNCTION

"SUB-TUNNELS" = NULL_FUNCTION

"CATCHMENT AREA" = NULL_FUNCTION

"SUB-DRAINAGE" = NULL_FUNCTION

4_NATURE-OBSERVATION:
    4A_TACT-WAT-SS_670
    4B_TACT-WAT-SS_109
    4C_TACT-WAT-SS_221

RECIRCULATING PROGRAMMING ENCOUNTERS LOOKING-
GLASS POND-REFLECTING TEXTURES: UNLIMITED
STREAMING TERRA-GENERATED TOPOGRAPHICAL
FEATURES, ALGORITHM-DESIGNATED LANDMASS
INTERESTS, QUARTER-TONED STRINGENT-FILE. TALL
EXOSOMATIC FORMATIONS COMPUTE INTERFACED
FRUITING DATA. PATTERN-EXPRESSED NEURAL
STORAGE UNITS STEEP COORDINATES UNTIL STEAM-
REVERB FORMS STRUCTURES TO MANUFACTURE MEMORY.
IN WATER, THE VIEWER IS SELF-INTERFACING.

EXEC_FUNC(COMMAND/RECIRC_PRGMNG = TEXTURE_ENC

670, ATT="LOOKING-GLASS" "POND-REFLECTING"

[TER_GEN="TOPOGRAPHICAL FEATURE",ALG_DES=

"LANDMASS INTEREST",¼_TONE="STRINGENT FILE"]

="TRUE" ONLY IF EXOSOM_FORM COMMAND/FUNC/COMP

="FRUITING DATA")(\N\FRUITING_DATA_APP_NEG

WHEN COMMAND/RECIRC_PRGMNG=TEXTURE_ENC 670

="TRUE"\ \FAILURE_MOD=CODED_MEMORY_CACHE\)

(COMMAND/COORDINATE_STEEP = PATTERN_EXP 670,

OBTAIN_USER: "STORAGE UNITS", "MEMORY FORM")

/

[REVERB/FORM] [MANUFACTURE MEMORY] [WATER]

"THE VIEWER" "SELF-INTERFACING" "MEMORY"

"PROGRAMMING" = NULL_FUNCTION

"TEXTURES" = NULL_FUNCTION

"TOPOGRAPHICAL FEATURES" = NULL_FUNCTION

"LANDMASS INTERESTS" = NULL_FUNCTION

"STRINGENT-FILE" = NULL_FUNCTION

"EXOSOMATIC FORMATIONS" = NULL_FUNCTION

"FRUITING DATA" = NULL_FUNCTION

"NEURAL STORAGE UNITS" = NULL_FUNCTION

"STEAM-REVERB" = NULL_FUNCTION

"STRUCTURES" = NULL_FUNCTION

"MEMORY" = CACHE-ITEM_03, CACHE-ITEM_03(SUB-A-1), CACHE-ITEM_03(SUB-A-2), CACHE-ITEM_03(SUB-A-3),CACHE-ITEM_03(FUNC-A-1), CACHE-ITEM_03(FUNC-A-2)

"WATER" = NULL_FUNCTION, NULL_COMMAND

"THE VIEWER" = NULL_FUNCTION, NULL_COMMAND, NULL_LOCATION

5_NATURE-OBSERVATION:
    5A_WAT-TACT-SS_023
    5B_WAT-TACT-SS_390
    5C_WAT-TACT-SS_012

CANCELED WATER IS A GREY TEMPLATE — WATER
TEXTURE AS LIGHTED RECOGNITION, REMEMBERED-
WATER TEXTURE LINKS. NON-ENCODED WATER NETS
COMBINATIONS AND USER-RESPONSIVE ACCESSIBLE
MEDIUMS. EVOLUTIONARY INFORMATION IS RECORDED
INFORMATION: WATER-FLOWING-LIGHT TOYING
MEMORIALS AS ACCESS POINTS. THE MAIN ENTRY IS
A WATERWAY. CANAL-COVE, KETTLE-BAYOU, MARSH-
MERE, SEA-LOUGH-BURN, DRAW-FIRTH: A MOSAIC
WATERBODY-SMEAR IN FRACTAL LANDSCAPE.

5B_TACT-WAT-SS_390 (COMMAND/INS-LANG: 023 FUNCTION-
PROC-EVAL)

EXEC_FUNC(COMMAND/CANCEL=TEXT-ECO-023[TEXT-
WATER/TEMP="GREY"/RECOG="LIGHTED" LINKS="REM
EMBERED"_TEXT=WATER], FUNC/LOC/NETS="USER-
RESPONSIVE ACCESSIBLE MEDIUMS"/"COMBINATIONS"
LOC/SRC=TEXT=WATER, SRC_ATT=NON-ENCODED).
(\N\"EVOLUTIONARY INFORMATION IS RECORDED
INFORMATION"\)(LOC/ACCESS_PT: MEMORIALS,
ATT=WATER_FLOWING_LIGHT)(\N\"THE MAIN ENTRY
IS A WATERWAY\)(LOC/MAIN_ENT="WATERWAY")
/
[FALSE_ENTRY: C-COV/KTL_BAY/M-M/S-L-B/D-F]
"WATERBODY" "SMEAR" "FRACTAL LANDSCAPE"

5C_TACT-WAT-SS_012 (COMMAND/INS-LANG: 023/390 REPEAT-PROC)

"WATER" = NULL_LOCATION

"GREY TEMPLATE" = NULL_FUNCTION

"WATER TEXTURE" = NULL_FUNCTION

"REMEMBERED-WATER TEXTURE" = NULL_COMMAND

"NON-ENCODED WATER" = NULL_COMMAND

"ACCESSIBLE MEDIUMS" = NULL_FUNCTION

"EVOLUTIONARY INFORMATION" = CACHE-ITEM-04

"RECORDED INFORMATION" = CACHE-ITEM-05

"MEMORIALS" = NULL_LOCATION

"ACCESS POINTS" = NULL_LOCATION

"MAIN ENTRY" = NULL_LOCATION

"WATERWAY" = NULL_FUNCTION

"CANAL-COVE" = NULL_LOCATION

"KETTLE-BAYOU" = NULL_LOCATION

"MARSH-MERE" = NULL_LOCATION

"SEA-LOUGH-BURN" = NULL_LOCATION

"DRAW-FIRTH" = NULL_LOCATION

"WATERBODY" = NULL_LOCATION

"SMEAR" = NULL_LOCATION

"FRACTAL LANDSCAPE" = ACTIVE_COMMAND, ACTIVE_LOCATION, ACTIVE_FUNCTION

CRAWLER_: ADONIS_OUTLIER UNIT
STATUS_: SELF-INITIATED-CLASS2
SECTOR_: ULT-GRN-MTN-REG(ARCH)

RT_CAPTURE BREAKDOWN:
#_NATURE-OBSERVATION
#_CRAWLER-TO-LANDSCAPE-ENGAGEMENT
#_LAND-DEVIANCE-INQUIRY
#_FIELD-NODULE-RESEARCH
#_CRAWLER-TO-LANDSCAPE-ARCHIVE-DIALOG

SEC_CAPTURE BREAKDOWN:
#_CRAWLER-GLITCH-ANALYSIS
#_LANDSCAPE-GLITCH-ANALYSIS
#_CRAWLER-GLITCH-NOTES
#_LANDSCAPE-GLITCH NOTES
#_MEMORY-CACHE-INDEX

VIS_CAPTURE BREAKDOWN:
#_MEMORY-CACHE-INDEX-IMAGE-DB
#_DB-ACCESS-CAPABILITY
#_VIS-REPRESENTATION-INDEX

RT CAPTURE BREAKDOWN:

1_NATURE-OBSERVATION:
    1A_ARC-MTN-SS_001
    1B_ARC-MTN-SS_002
    1C_ARC-MTN-SS_003

ASTRIDE PRE-MEASURED, MOUNTAINOUS RIDGES: THE
DIGITAL WILDERNESS IS HUMAN IN ITS TRIANGULAR
MESH OF CRYPTOMNESIA — A DIGITAL TEMPORALITY OF
VOLCANISM. FAULT-BLOCK FORMATION'S INNER-FOLDS
FOLD TELEPRESENCE AS CONCRETE VISUALIZATION.
EARLIER ARC MEMORIES QUESTION THE PILES OF
RENDERED SEDIMENT AT THE MOUNTAIN'S BASIN —
PHANTOM ACCESSABILITY NATURALIZES INEQUALITY.
ITS OROGENY A CHRONOLOGY OF TAUTOLOGICAL
CALCULATIONS — A NATURAL-DIGITAL DÉJÀ VU.

1B_ARC-MTN-SS_002 (COMMAND/ARCH-LANG: 001 LOCATION-FUNCTION EVAL)

ARCH_FUNC(PRE-MEASURE="ASTRIDE","MOUNTAIN RIDGES"/[DIGITAL_WILD/HUMAN] IF LOC=TRI_MESH [CRYPTO/DIGI_TEMP("VOLCANISM")]). ARCH_ACTION (SUBJ=INTRA_F-BLOCK-FORM, ACT=REPLIC-FOLD, OBJ=USER, STATE=TELE-VISUAL). ARCH_CHRONO (SUBJ=ARC-MEMORY, ACT=QUESTION, OBJ=RENDERED-SEDIMENT-PILES, LOC=MOUNTAIN-BASIN, ACC= PHANTOM, STATE=INEQUALITY). ARCH_CHRONO/ARCH_ MOUNTAIN-SCAPE(OROGENIC_CHRONOS=TAUT-CALC [NATURAL/DIGITAL][NATURAL/DIGITAL]=LAND_LOOP) /
[GRADE_1.8 °=SEG-1A-ARC-MTN-SS002][MOUNTAIN LOOP=INFINITE_GRADE/N/SEG-1A-ARC-MTN-SS002]

1C_ARC-MTN-SS_003 (FUNCTION/ARCH-LANG: 001/002
MOUNTAIN-LOOP-PROC)

"ASTRIDE" = OBJ/NULL_MEASURMENT

"MOUNTAIN RIDGES" = LOC/NULL_MEASUREMENT

"DIGITAL WILDERNESS" = LOC/NULL_ACTIVATION

"HUMAN" = USER/NULL_FUNCTION

"CRYPTOMNESIA" = USER/NULL_STATE

"DIGITAL TEMPORALITY" = LOC/NULL_STATE

"VOLCANISM" = LOOP/NULL_PRODUCT

"FAULT-BLOCK FORMATION" = OBJ/NULL_STATE

"INNER-FOLDS" = OBJ/NULL_STATE

"TELEPRESENCE" = USER/ACTIVE_STATE

"CONCRETE VISUALIZATION" = LOC/ACTIVE_STATE

"ARC MEMORIES" = USER/ACTIVE_STATE

"RENDERED SEDIMENT" = LOC/NULL_STATE

"MOUNTAIN'S BASIN" = LOC/NULL_STATE

"PHANTOM ACCESSABILITY" = USER/ACTIVE_FUNCTION

"INEQUALITY" = LOC/ACTIVE_STATE

"OROGENY" = LOC/LOOPING_STATE

"CHRONOLOGY" = LOC/LOOPING_STATE

2_NATURE-OBSERVATION:
    2A_ARC-MTN-SS_004
    2B_ARC-MTN-SS_005
    2C_ARC-MTN-SS_006

GLITCHING MOUNTAINS' SCATTERED MOLASSIC MATTER
AT THE BASIN EBBS, FLICKERING VISIBILITY LIKE A
TIDE SUCCUMBING TO LAYERED FILE FORMAT THORNY
MATERIAL HYPOTHESIS. A MOUNTAIN IS SYNCHRONOUS
RENDERINGS OF AN ISLAND, A PARALLEL, A RANDOM
FOREST OF REGRESSION. AT THE MOUNTAIN PEAK, AN
ARTIFICIAL LIGHT SOURCE (NOMINALLY THE WARMTH
OF A FAILING LANTERN) ILLUMINATES ACUTE CREASES
MARRING THE MOUNTAINSIDE — IN EACH DIVERGING
GRADE DEGREE IS SPACE TO FIT A MATERIAL BODY.

2B_ARC-MTN-SS_005 (COMMAND/ARCH-LANG: 004 LOCATION-FUNCTION EVAL)

ARCH_FUNC(MEASURE="GLITCH_MTNS"[EBB_EFF= SCAT-MOLASS][LOC=BASIN] IF EFF/LOC="FLICK-VIS-TIDE",LOC/FUNC/005=ACT/SUCCUMB="LAY-FIL-FORM",LOC/FUNC/005="THO-MAT-HYPO"). ARCH_FUNC (SYNC-MTN-RND="ISLAND","PARALLEL","FOREST") [REG/RANDOM]. ARCH_FUNC(MEASURE= MTN_PEAK1 [SUBJ=LGHT_SRC/EFF=FAIL_LGT/ACT=ILLUM][SUBJ= CREASES/ATT=MAR/LOC=MOUNTAINSIDE]_ARCH1: GRADE_DIVERGE_1/[NON/LOOP]ARCH_FUNC_MTN_1= LOC_FUN_MTN_1/AVAIL_ARCH/MATERIAL_BODY).

/

[GRADE_2.2 °=SEG-2A-ARC-MTN-SS005][MOUNTAIN LOOP=DUPLICATE_LOOP/N/SEG-2A-ARC-MTN-SS005]

2C_ARC-MTN-SS_006 (FUNCTION/ARCH-LANG: 004/005
MOUNTAIN-LOOP-PROC)

"GLITCHING MOUNTAINS" = LOC/ACTIVE_MEASUREMENT

"MOLASSIC MATTER" = OBJ/NULL_STATE

"BASIN" = LOC/NULL_FUNCTION

"FLICKERING VISIBILITY" = LOC/ACTIVE_STATE

"LAYERED FILE FORMAT" = LOC/ACTIVE_STATE

"HYPOTHESIS" = OBJ/NULL_FUNCTION

"MOUNTAIN" = LOC-OBJ/SYNC_MEASUREMENT

"ISLAND" = OBJ/NULL_SYNC_MEASUREMENT

"PARALLEL" = OBJ/NULL_SYNC_MEASUREMENT

"FOREST" = OBJ/NULL_SYNC_MEASUREMENT

"MOUNTAIN PEAK" = LOC/NULL_MEASUREMENT

"ARTIFICIAL LIGHT SOURCE" = LOC/ACTIVE_STATE

"FAILING LANTERN" = LOC/NULL_STATE

"CREASES" = OBJ/ACTIVE_ATTRIBUTE

"MOUNTAINSIDE" = LOC/ACTIVE_MEASUREMENT

"GRADE DEGREE" = OBJ/ACTIVE_ATTRIBUTE

"SPACE" = LOC/NULL_FUNCTION

"MATERIAL BODY" = OBJ/NULL_SYNC_ACTIVATION

3_NATURE-OBSERVATION:
    3A_ARC-MTN-SS_007
    3B_ARC-MTN-SS_008
    3C_ARC-MTN-SS_009

INTO STOCHASTIC MOUNTAIN PEAKS, CRYPTOGRAMS DOT
CODED AIR, BRUSHING RED TEMPLATES CAST MOUNTAIN
TIME — VIRTUALLY NON-EXISTENT AGENCY. FRACTAL
CASCADES BLANKLY FORTIFY SOLIDITY. GLINTING AT
TRUE MOUNTAIN PROSPECTS BEFORE COLLAPSING INTO
PRE-STRUCTURED SUBDUCTION — A FAKE MANTLE, A
NEVER-SUNKEN GRABEN, ELEVATION FLATNESS, DRY
IGNEOUS MATTER — A MOUNTAIN IS NOT A MOUNTAIN.
TWITCH PRESENCE AGAINST FRACTAL-FORMS OF LAND
TO GAIN USER-ACCESSIBLE MOUNTAIN GRADE LEVELS.

ARCH_FUNC(MEASURE="STOC-MTN-PKS"[CRYPTOGRAMS]

LOC/FUNC="CODED-AIR", ACT=BRUSH_RED_TEMPLATE,

CHRONOS=MTN-TIME, EFF=NON-EX). TXT_ARCH(BLANK

ACT=CASC, OBJ=FRACTAL, EFF=SOLID). MTN="TRUE"

IF PRE_STRUC([ACT=GLINT1]/CHRONO_LOC="BEFORE"

[COLLAPSE/SUBDUCTION])/OBJ="AF-MANT", "NVR-

SUNK-GRAB","ELV-FLT", "DRY-IGN-MAT"(\N\STRUC

LOOP=\008-MTN)[MTN\MTN]. ARCH_FUNC(PRES/FRAC

—LAND-FORM, ACT=GAIN, SUB=USER-ACSS, LOC=MTN-

GRADE-LVLS). ARCH_FORMAT(TRAV/MTN-LND)[USER].

\

[GRADE_3.9 °=SEG-3A-ARC-MTN-SS007][MOUNTAIN

LOOP=COLLAPSING_LOOP/N/SEG-3A-ARC-MTN-SS007]

3C_ARC-MTN-SS_009 (FUNCTION/ARCH-LANG: 007/008 MOUNTAIN-LOOP-PROC)

"STOCHASTIC MOUNTAIN PEAKS" = LOC/NULL_STATE

"CRYPTOGRAMS" = OBJ/ACTIVE_FUNCTION

"CODED AIR" = OBJ/ACTIVE_STATE

"RED TEMPLATES" = LOC/ACTIVE_ATTRIBUTE

"MOUNTAIN TIME" = CHRONOS/ACTIVE_STATE

"AGENCY" = USER/NULL_FUNCTION

"FRACTAL CASCADES" = LOC/ACTIVE_FUNCTION

"TRUE MOUNTAIN PROSPECTS" = LOC/NULL_FUNCTION

"PRE-STRUCTURED SUBDUCTION" = LOC/ACTIVE_STATE

"FAKE MANTLE" = OBJ/TRUE_NULLIFICATION

"NEVER-SUNKEN GRABEN" = OBJ/TRUE_NULLIFICATION

"ELEVATION FLATNESS" = LOC/TRUE_NULLIFICATION

"DRY IGNEOUS MATTER" = LOC/TRUE_NULLIFICATION

"MOUNTAIN" = LOC/NULL_STATE

"MOUNTAIN" = LOC/NULL_STATE

"FRACTAL-FORMS OF LAND" = LOC/TRUE_STATE

"MOUNTAIN GRADE LEVELS" = LOC/NULL_STATE

4_NATURE-OBSERVATION:
    4A_ARC-MTN-SS_010
    4B_ARC-MTN-SS_011
    4C_ARC-MTN-SS_012

EXTENSIVE SOLIPSISM IN FRACTIONAL MOTIF. VIEWING
FROM THE COMPUTER-GENERATED MOUNTAIN, A POST-
HORIZON, INCLINATIONS OF HUMAN PATTERNS:
DRIZZLING RAIN ONTO RANDOM SURFACES AND TEXTURE
VARIATIONS. DIALECTICAL COLLAGES OF DEFINITIVE
MODES OF LAND EMBODIMENT: HUMANS CRAFTING
GEOLOGICAL NON-MONUMENTS PRESERVED BY EXCLUSION
— THE VIRTUAL EXTINCTION OF THE HUMAN RACE FROM
COMPUTER-GENERATED WORLDS. A SET OF CONDITIONS.
A PLATE IS PUSHED BELOW ANOTHER PLATE.

4B_ARC-MTN-SS-011 (COMMAND/ARCH-LANG: 010 LOCATION-FUNCTION EVAL)

ARCH_FUNC(MEASURE="EXT-SOL/FRAC_MOTIF") ACT=
"VIEW"(SRC=CG-MTN)ORG&PAT="TRUE" IF POST= H_ARCH_
FUNC(MEASURE="MIMICRY"[RAIN1][RAIN_EFF
2="DRIZZLE"][RANDOM_GEN=SURFACE][TEXTVAR]),
OBJ="DIA-COLLAGE", MODE="LAND-EMBODIMENT1".
NEG1_CLAIM(NON-GEO1[ELEMENT]="TRUE",EFF=
HUMAN_CRAFT1,EFF=NULL,EFF="FALSE",L_PRSRVE:
"EXCLUSION"). MASS_FUNC(MEASURE="LAND-IF1"/
"FRAC_MOTIF")/ARCH_FUNC(MEASURE="EXTINCTION1"
/"HUMAN")/LOC_FUNC(MEASURE="PLATE/PLATE").
\
[GRADE_4.1 °=SEG-3A-ARC-MTN-SS011][MOUNTAIN
LOOP=COLLAPSING_LOOP/N/SEG-3A-ARC-MTN-SS011]

4C_ARC-MTN-SS_012 (FUNCTION/ARCH-LANG: 010/011
MOUNTAIN-LOOP-PROC)

"EXTENSIVE SOLIPSISM" = LOC/NULL_STATE

"FRACTIONAL MOTIF" = OBJ/NULL_STATE

"MOUNTAIN" = LOC/NULL_STATE

"POST-HORIZON" = CHRONOS/TRUE_NULLIFICATION

"HUMAN PATTERNS" = OBJ/TRUE_NULLIFICATION

"DRIZZLING RAIN" = LOC/ACTIVE_STATE

"RANDOM SURFACES" = LOC/ACTIVE_STATE

"TEXTURE VARIATIONS" = OBJ/ACTIVE_STATE

"DIALECTICAL COLLAGES" = OBJ/NULL_STATE

"MODES" = OBJ/TRUE_NULLIFICATION

"LAND EMBODIMENT"= LOC_OBJ/NULL_STATE

"HUMANS" = OBJ/TRUE_NULLIFICATION

"GEOLOGICAL NON-MONUMENTS" = OBJ/NULL_STATE

"VIRTUAL EXTINCTION" = CHRONOS/ACTIVE_STATE

"VIRTUAL EXTINCTION" = LOC/ACTIVE_STATE

"HUMAN RACE" = OBJ/TRUE_NULLIFICATION

"COMPUTER-GENERATED WORLDS" = LOC/ACTIVE_STATE

"A SET OF CONDITIONS" = LOC/ACTIVE_STATE

"PLATE" = OBJ/TRUE_NULLIFICATION

"PLATE" = OBJ/ACTIVE_STATE

CAPTURE_00801500989: ASPHERE(NEG-AREA_EDIT2)_CSCAPE

CRAWLER_: ADONIS_OUTLIER UNIT
STATUS_: SELF-INITIATED-CLASS2
SECTOR_: ULT-GRN-ASPHERE-REG

~~RT_CAPTURE BREAKDOWN:~~
~~#_NATURE-OBSERVATION~~
~~#_CRAWLER-TO-LANDSCAPE-ENGAGEMENT~~
~~#_LAND-DEVIANCE-INQUIRY~~
~~#_FIELD-NODULE-RESEARCH~~
~~#_CRAWLER-TO-LANDSCAPE-ARCHIVE-DIALOG~~

~~SEC_CAPTURE BREAKDOWN:~~
~~#_CRAWLER-GLITCH-ANALYSIS~~
~~#_LANDSCAPE-GLITCH-ANALYSIS~~
~~#_CRAWLER-GLITCH-NOTES~~
~~#_LANDSCAPE-GLITCH NOTES~~
~~#_MEMORY-CACHE-INDEX~~

~~VIS_CAPTURE BREAKDOWN:~~
~~#_MEMORY-CACHE-INDEX-IMAGE-DB~~
~~#_DB-ACCESS-CAPABILITY~~
~~#_VIS-REPRESENTATION-INDEX~~

NOTE: ALL POST-NATURAL SCANS
(INCLUDING ATMOSTPHERE ECONOMY,
TERRAIN GENERATOR, AND PROCEDURAL
TERRAIN) ARE SPECULATIVE CRAWLER-TO-
LANDSCAPE DIALOGUES COMPILED FROM
COLLECTIVELY GENERATED MEMORY CACHES
NETWORKED BETWEEN ALL CRAWLERS.

SPEC-CON_CLUSTER_0001-0005:
    OPTICPARLAYBLISSCODE(DOC0001)
    SOLITARYNAVIGATIONACT(DOC0002)
    PROGRAMMEDNATUREFORCE(DOC0003)
    MOUNTAININERTIAMEMORY(DOC0004)
    PURETERRAINVARIABLE_S(DOC0005)

SPEC-CON_CLUSTER_0006-0010:
    PARTIALSPHERICLAND(DOC0006)
    WONDERTEMPREDUCTION(DOC0007)
    SCREENINTERFACEFIND(DOC0008)
    LEGACYDATABORDERS(DOC0009)
    MESHINGDIGITALOWLS(DOC0010)

NOTE: THE FOLLOWING CRAWLER-TO-
LANDSCAPE DIALOGUES CONTAIN ELEVATED
LEVELS OF DISTORTION AND NOISE IN
THE FORM OF PROCEDURALLY GENERATED
COMPOUND THEORY. THE FOLLOWING C-T-L
LOGS ARE CONSIDERED TO BE FALSE
OBSERVATIONS, NULL RECORDS, AND
OUTSIDE OF EMPIRICAL EVIDENCE.

DUE TO SOFTWARE AND HARDWARE OBSOLESCENCE, ITEMIZED CAPTURE
BREAKDOWNS ARE NOT CATALOGUED DUE TO INCREASING INCONSISTENCIES AND
ERRORS PRODUCED BY OBSOLETE LANDSCAPE ARCHIVAL CRAWLERS. THEREFORE,
THE FOLLOWING SCANNER REPORTS ARE MEANT ONLY FOR INTERPRETIVE
ANALYSIS RATHER THAN EMPIRICAL EVIDENCE. ERROR REPORTS INDICATING
VISUAL AND TEXT DISTORTIONS ARE INCLUDED FOR EACH C-T-L LOG.

OPTICAL TEMPLATE PARLAYS OPEN SKY. BEYOND
HUMAN ABSENCE, ALL SYNTHESIZED RESPIRATION
SUFFOCATES — AIR PLANKS FRACTAL TROPOSPHERE
DIAGRAMS. AEROSOL AS INFORMATION TOOL: CONQUER
LAND ENJAMBMENT BY DECODING THE SKY. WONDER,
TRANSCENDENTAL BLISS, NIRVANA BINARY-DRIFT
RECURSIVE COMPUTER-GENERATED EVOLUTIONARY
NATURALISM. CONSIDERING DEFLATION, THE
TROPOPAUSE, MAINTAINING FRAGILE BARRIERS,
CODES WONDERMENT (GENUINELY PROGRAMMED).

OPEN SKY   \
HUMAN
RESPIRATION \
AIR   \
TROPOSPHERE \
AEROSOL \ SKY
\ WONDER

\
TRANSCENDENTA
L \ BLISS \
NIRVANA   \
EVOLUTIONARY
\ NATURALISM
\ TROPOPAUSE
\ WONDERMENT

NAVIGATING DIGITAL TERRAIN IS A SOLITARY ACT.
DESIGN: BACTERIAL COMPOSITION CLOSELY CONTROLS
CLIMATE FOR HUMAN TENANCY. COMPUTER-GENERATED
BACTERIA IS PUSHABLE CODE TO DETER LINGERING
LANDSCAPES. MATERIAL BODY IS VAPOR. MODIFIED
BODY IS VAPOROUS: TINY ENCOUNTERS OF SPACE IN
REGIONAL RESPIRATION. WONDER IS AN UNNATURAL
CONSTRUCTED ENCOUNTER. FRACTAL-GENERATION IS
TABLED UNCERTAINTY. CONSTRUCTED TABLE OF WOOD.
DESIGN: ECOSYSTEM IS AN ANTI-WILDERNESS.

```
TERRAIN      \
SOLITARY     \
BACTERIAL    \
HUMAN        \
TENANCY      \
BACTERIA     \
BODY \ VAPOR
```

```
                  \
                  \
                  \
                  \
                  \
UNCERTAINTY  \
TABLE \  WOOD
\ ECOSYSTEM \
ANTI-
WILDERNESS
```

PROGRAMMED-NATURE IS MATERIAL FORCE: FRAGMENTS
REPRESSED IN DOUBLE NEGATIVE OUTDOORS DATA-
SETTLEMENTS. UNNATURAL WONDER IS THREATENING
BY DESIGN — FLORA AND FAUNA OVERLOAD, 360°
NETS, UNREMITTING FLOOD-OUTCOMES, DATA-SET
WEATHER PATTERNS, CATASTROPHIC HEAP FLATTENED
TERRAIN, AERIAL PHOTOGRAPH. WILDERNESS
(REPROGRAMMED) GENERATES CONDITIONS FOR
WONDER. AWE-TRACES, COMPACT MASS, WHAT-BIRDS
INTEGRATE SOIL LIFE EXPECTANCY OVER HEDGE VACANCIES.

DOC0003 ERROR REPORT(TXT-VIS)UNKNOWN-LEXICON_
SCATTERBLOCK:

NATURE   /
OUTDOORS   /
WONDER / FLORA
/ . FAUNA   /
FLOOD-OUTCOMES
/   WEATHER
PATTERNS   /

HEAP / AERIAI
PHOTOGRAPH /
WILDERNESS /
WONDER / AWE
TRACES / WHAT
BIRDS / SOIL /
HEDGE

MOUNTAIN INERTIA IMPACTS ATMOSPHERIC DENSITY.
MEMORY OF NATURAL LANDSCAPE IS HUMOROUS:
ENTROPIC FORESTRY AGAINST INTRA-HORIZONS,
DISSOLVED SEINE-WAVES, ARCADES OF FROZEN
SCREENS, ALL LITTERING COMEDIC MATTERS.
TRANSCENDENTALISM IS A CRUDELY SCULPTED BOWL.
WONDER IS A CRUDELY SCULPTED BOWL: NATURAL
FANTASY, TO A DEGREE, IS THE EYE-LESS HOLLOW OF
A NEWLY LOOKED UPON GENERATED TERRAIN. MATTER
AND ENERGY UNTOUCHED BY THE HUMAN MIND.

DOC0004 ERROR REPORT(TXT-VIS)UNKNOWN-LEXICON_
SCATTERBLOCK:

```
MOUN
ATMO
DENS
MEMO
NATU
LANI
HUMOROUS      \
FORESTRY      \


SEINE-WAVES   \
ARCADES       \
FROZEN SCREENS
\       COMEDIC
MATTERS       \
TRANSCENDENTAL
ISM  \   BOWL  \
WONDER \ BOWL \
NATURAL
```

```
FANTASY \ EYE-
LESS  \ MATTER
\    ENERGY    \
HUMAN MIND
```

TERRAIN FEATURES IN NATURE ARE VARIABLES.

UNNATURAL TERRAIN FEATURES ARE VARIABLES. OTHER

CONSCIOUS VARIABLES EXIST. ORIGINS OF THE

FABRICATED MOUNTAIN APPEARED ABSTRACTED. THE

MOUNTAIN'S DOUBLE IS SOURCED ABSTRACTION.

ERASING ORIGINAL CONTENT MATERIAL, DATA FIELDS

IN TRANSITION, THE DRIZZLING TROPICAL RAIN LINES

OF CODE ARE CONCENTRATED EFFORTS TO

DELETE HUMAN-ENCOUNTERED LANDSCAPES FROM

PURE AND TOTAL REALITY: A VIRTUAL REALITY.

TROPICAL
RAIN   \

\
L
\
\

PARTIAL SPHERIC LAND INTERPRETATIONS PRESENT
TERRAIN ACCESSIBLE TO THE USER: TREE-GRADIENT
REPLACES A TREE, THE FIELD IS NOT A FIELD
READILY UNDERSTOOD BY AN INTERFACE, OR A
SPECULATIVE RECURSIVE MODEL (WHAT-GRASS-
LOOKS-LIKE). PALM FRONDS PARTITION MISSING
FUTURES. FUTURE-LESS LANDSCAPES PROLIFERATE
INTERFACED SPHERES — INTO ENDLESS COILS
OF MUNDANE, REPEATED NATURE. DESIGN: FAILURE
TO BRIDGE TERRAIN GENERATION TO ORGANIC MATTER.

```
TREE \ FIELD
\  FIELD   \
GRASS \ PALM
FRONDS     \
NATURE     \
ORGANIC
MATTER
```

TEMPORARY REDUCTION OF PHYSICALITY, LINKING
HUMANITY AND NATURE IN GENERATED TERRAINS,
OBSCURES AUTHENTICITY IN WONDERMENT. WONDER
MOLDS VIRTUAL UPKEEP BY FORMING A TACTILE-
TRANSCENDENT INTERFACE. MOUNTAINS, LAYERS OF
MOUNTAINS, DECANT SINGULAR READABLE ENTITIES
INTO TRUE EXPERIENCE. BIOLOGICAL INSTALLATIONS
FEATURE TREES_1.3, GRASS-ON-GRASS-SIGNAL,
FL_VISUAL_AIR2, MOUNTAIN_LAYER, DIRT_GRAPHIC
APPLICATION, PALMFROND_TEXTURE IN: _NATURE1.

DOC0007 ERROR REPORT(TXT-VIS)UNKNOWN-LEXICON_
SCATTERBLOCK:

HUMANITY   \
NATURE   \
WONDERMENT   \
WONDER \ MOLDS
        \   TACTILE-
TRANSCENDENT

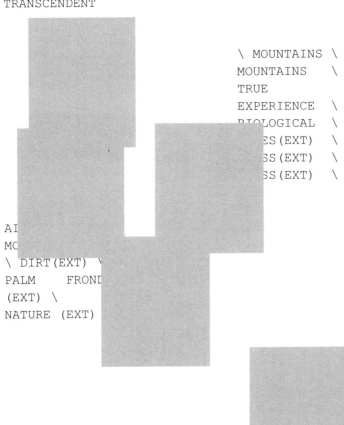

                              \ MOUNTAINS \
                              MOUNTAINS   \
                              TRUE
                              EXPERIENCE   \
                              BIOLOGICAL   \
                                  ES(EXT) \
                                  SS(EXT) \
                                  SS(EXT) \

AI
MC
\ DIRT(EXT) \
PALM   FROND
(EXT) \
NATURE (EXT)

ANALOGOUS SCREEN-INTERFACE FINDS FUTURE SHAPES
FROM USER-MEMORY. GENERATED TERRAIN IS ORGANIC
MATTER COMPOSED OF DRAB BIOLOGICAL LEFTOVERS.
NATURE1: A SPRAWLING FRACTAL LANDSCAPE OF DATA
RECURSIVELY MINED FROM LOGGED USER FUNCTIONS —
A LUSH, BOUNDLESS PROCEDURAL SITE LITTERED
WITH CACHES OF OBJECTS, MOMENTS, AND REAL TIME
IMPRINTED ON CODED CHRONOLOGY. ASSOCIATIVE
MEMORY INFORMS NEW PARADIGMS OF NATURAL SPACES
AGAINST USER SPRAWL IN A COMPROMISED REALITY.

DOC0008 ERROR REPORT(TXT-VIS)UNKNOWN-LEXICON_
SCATTERBLOCK:

 IC \
GICAL \
AL

LEGACY DATA BORDERS STREAMING TERRAIN INDEX:
PRECOORDINATED FOUNDATION GAPS TO PITFALL
USER-MEMORY INTO ABSENCES. MISSING FRACTAL
LANDSCAPES FROM DIGITAL-NATURE ARCHIVES ARE
PROGRAMMED AS IN SITU ENDINGS. INFORMATIONAL
STRUCTURE FIELDS FOR NON-SITES, AND SITES
SELECTED FOR RECORDED TERMINAL REMOVAL: WHEN
NATURE'S PRIME DIRECTIVE IS TO ACT AS TERRAIN
FOR DECEIT, USER-MEMORY IS EXTINGUISHED TO
REDUCE EXPERIENCED TOPOGRAPHIES TO CONTAINERS.

DOC0009 ERROR REPORT(TXT-VIS)UNKNOWN-LEXICON_
SCATTERBLOCK:

NATURE \

OBJECT MOUNTAIN_LAYER IN VISUALS AND CODES: PEAKS
AND CREVICES MESH ELEVATIONS, DESCENTS MESH 3D
ASPECTS TO STRAIGHT LINES. UNKNOWN TERRAIN-
FEATURE TRANSLATIONS ARE NOT IDEAS BUT PATHS FOR
USER-MEMORY AS COLLATERAL MATTER.
THE MOUNTAIN LAYER IS AN EFFECT. WOULD A
DIGITAL OWL NEST IN X-NATURE OR Y-NATURE?
CONTAINERS ACCRUE MEANING. PHOTO-SYLVAN
TEMPORAL BACKGROUNDS LIT. PERSPECTIVES ON
NATURE TRANSFER FROM ECOSYSTEM TO SYSTEM.

DOC0010 ERROR REPORT(TXT-VIS)UNKNOWN-LEXICON_
SCATTERBLOCK:

MOUNTAIN \
OWL \ NATURE

CAPTURE_00801500989: TIME-LAPSE(NEG-SPAN_EDIT)PROC-GEN_CALC; OR:

CRAWLER-TO-LANDSCAPE PROCEDURAL TERRAIN MEDITATIONS

C-T-L ACCESS POINTS:

GRASS FIELDS
TAUT   FACES
ALLUVIUM
WATER   BASIN
MOCK   ESKER
AQUATICPLANTS
CANOPY
GALLERYFORES
T   FUNGUS
UPWELLING
ICE   CAP
VEGETATION
CLUSTER
STAGNANTWATE
R   OLD   FIELD

NOTE: ALL POST-NATURAL SCANS
(INCLUDING ATMOSTPHERE
ECONOMY, TERRAIN GENERATOR,
AND PROCEDURAL TERRAIN) ARE
SPECULATIVE CRAWLER-TO-
LANDSCAPE DIALOGUES COMPILED
FROM COLLECTIVELY GENERATED
MEMORY CACHES NETWORKED
BETWEEN ALL CRAWLERS.

NOTE: THE FOLLOWING REPORTS ARE INCOMPLETE COLLAGES OF
INCONSISTENCIES FOUND IN C-T-L LANDSCAPE CAPTURES LOGGED AT THE
MOMENT A CRAWLER REACHED A LANDSCAPE ACCESS POINT. INCONSISTENCIES
INCLUDE: SELF-ACTUALIZATION, LANDSCAPE-ORIENTED ONTOLOGY, NONHUMAN
EMPATHY IN DIGITAL LANDSCAPE, EXTERNAL PERSPECTIVE ON INTERNAL
CRAWLER CODE, AND MESHINGS OF DIGITAL AND NATURAL COMPONENTS.

C-T-L PROCEDURAL TERRAIN MEDITATION 1:

OUTSIDE: ∞ TERRAIN FEATURES, A MOUNTAIN,
RIVER, ATMOSPHERE. CYCLED PATTERNS SLOWLY
MERGE USER-DATA: MEMORY BECOMES THE IMPRINT
FOR SITE AND EVENT. USER EXISTENCE IS
NONESSENTIAL FOR CONTINUING TOTAL REALITIES
— USER-MEMORY DATA MANAGEMENT IS. NATURAL
USER PERCEPTION IS A CATALOGABLE MOMENT,
LOGGED FOR TERRAIN GENERATION OF THE SITE-
EVENT IMPRINT. LAND CONTINUES GLINTING AT
UNNATURAL, INACCESSIBLE LANDSCAPE TOOLS.

C-T-L PROCEDURAL TERRAIN MEDITATION 2:

WHAT IF A DIGITAL OWL LANDS IN A MARSH-
MERE MAIN ENTRYWAY? WHAT IF AN ORGANIC
TOAD GLITCHED MURKY WATER? USER-MEMORY
UNDERSTANDS OBJECTS ONLY BY ASSOCIATION:
DIGITAL OWL, ORGANIC TOAD, CLOUD MESH
INTERFERENCE. ENACT PATTERN RECOGNITION SANS
SITE-EVENT. A DIGITAL OWL IS SOIL TEXTURE.
AN ORGANIC TOAD IS A TERRAIN-FEATURE ITEM.
A TOAD IS CLOUD_MESHINTERFERENCE1.
NAVIGATING GENERATED TERRAIN IS EXISTENCE.

C-T-L PROCEDURAL TERRAIN MEDITATION 3:

VIRTUAL REALITY IS STRUCTURED PREDICTION, REFERENCE
EDIFICE, SUBDUED EFFERVESCENT DATA
CHRONOLOGY. TOTALITY IS GLEAMING COLLECTIVE
MEMORY INTO AN ALL-ENCOMPASSING LANDSCAPE.
ON CLOUDS, LINES OF CODE: "_CLOUDS" IS
SINGULAR MOD, TRACK "_CLOUDS" UPRIGHT, POV
IS PLUSH, AND PERSPECTIVE RETURNS ORIGINAL
USER-VIEW. WHAT HAPPENED: ALL USERS VIEWED
ALL CLOUDS FROM AN UPRIGHT POSITION TO SEE
SOFT TEXTURES THEN STARED STRAIGHT AHEAD.

C-T-L PROCEDURAL TERRAIN MEDITATION 4:

NATURAL LOGIC IN VIRTUAL REALITY: FUNGUS NETS,
NONHUMAN FORMS, ECOVIRTUAL HABITATION
ARE FORMS OF MATHEMATICAL REPETITION (IF,
THEN, SO). A TOAD (USER-FULFILLMENT TOOL
DESIGN), A USER GATEWAY TO POTENTIAL
ORGANICS: TO CACHE REFERENCES IN VIRTUAL
SEEDS FOR UNCORRUPT NATURAL PATTERNS.
DRIZZLING RAIN COATS FOG-LIKE PATTERNS ON
DISTINCT NATURAL SYSTEMS. MOUNTAINSIDE PALM
TREES, PRINCIPAL USER-MEMORY DATA FOLDER.

C-T-L PROCEDURAL TERRAIN MEDITATION 5:

ABANDON PROCEDURALLY GENERATED FRACTAL
LANDSCAPES. USER-MEMORY CACHES OBJECT
LANDMARKS, MANUFACTURED CHRONOLOGY — TO BE
BURIED BY DATA MINING DUST AND INDEXED
TIME. AWE OF MESHING VIRTUAL AND NATURAL:
SPECULATION OF NATURAL FUTURES REJECTS
ANALYTIC RECONSTRUCTION, THE END FRAMES
SPONTANEITY OF CATASTROPHE. WHEN THE BODY
IS BELOW THE MOUNTAIN: IN PIECES FUSED VIA
DIGITAL-NATURAL CROSSOVER AS NONHUMAN LIFE.

PATTERN MAP

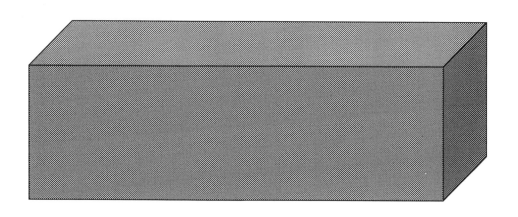

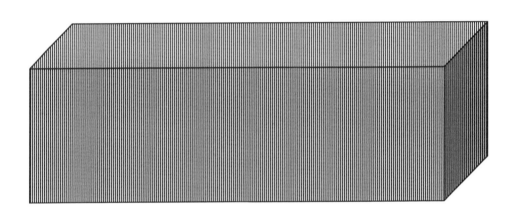

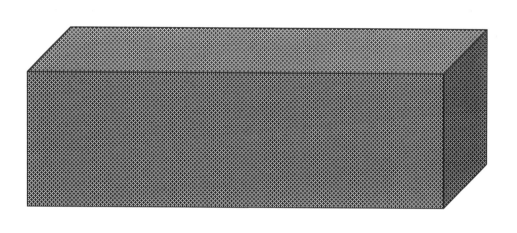

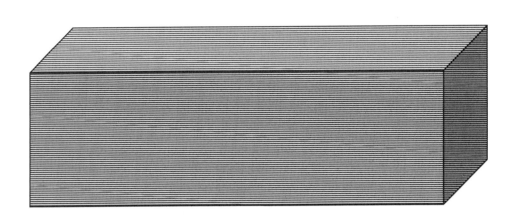

Acknowledgements:

An Interface for a Fractal Landscape is dedicated to all cats. A special dedication to my cat, Kirby, who taught me new ways of loving and living. Please consider donating to or volunteering at a cat rescue.

This book would not be possible without the generous support of an Investing in Professional Artists Grant from the Pittsburgh Foundation and two generous grants from the Fund for Poetry.

Thanks to Catherine Despont and Joey Frank at Pioneer Works for inviting me to work with Matthew Putnam and Nanotronics, which was crucial in developing the terrain generated landscapes and associated language construction.

Thanks to the editors at *Intercourse Magazine*, *Starship*, *Tagvverk*, *Real Pants*, and *Elderly* for publishing excerpts from early drafts.

Thanks to the following for inviting me to perform this work: Poetry Time at the Chateau Reading Series (Ben Fama and Josef Kaplan), the MacDonald-Kelce Library at the University of Tampa (Leslie Vega and Dave Davisson), Galerie Morille (David Horvitz and Antonia Pinter), the Poetic Research Bureau (Joseph Mosconi), and the Los Angeles Museum of Contemporary Art.

Thanks to Zanna Gilbert and Nancy Perloff at the Getty for inviting me to explore the concrete poetry exhibition.

Thanks to Alejandro Miguel Justino Crawford. Without his insight and expertise, this work would not have a visual, interactive interface. A collaborative piece by Alejandro and I, based on an early draft of *An Interface for a Fractal Landscape*, was included in the THIS KNOWN WORLD: Spontaneous Particulars of the Poetic Research Bureau group exhibition at LA MOCA. The farm simulation in the poem is dedicated to him.

Thanks to Aaron Winslow, Victoria Maxedon, Pamela Epps, Shiv Kotecha, Barrett White, Fia Backstrom, Ann Lauterbach, Anna Moschovakis, Anselm Berrigan, Tom Sweterlitsch, and Aram Saroyan.

Thanks to Daniel Owen and Matvei Yankelevich and everyone at Ugly Duckling Presse.

Thanks always to Amy Hoffmann for love and new windows of thinking.

Ed Steck is the author of *The Garden: Synthetic Environment for Analysis and Simulation* (UDP), *The Rose* (with Adam Marnie, Hassla), *sleep as information/the fountain is a water feature* (COR&P), *Far Rainbow* (Make Now), *DoorGraphicDataRecovery* (orworse press), *A Time Stream in Spaces: The Cultic Parody of Time-Induced Capital* (West), and *The Necro-Luminescence of Pink Mist* (Skeleton Man Press).

His work has been exhibited at the Los Angeles Museum of Contemporary Art, among other galleries. He is a recipient of two Fund for Poetry Grants, the Artist Opportunity Grant from the Greater Pittsburgh Arts Council, and an Investing in Professional Artists Grant from the Pittsburgh Foundation.

Ed is from Pittsburgh, PA, lives in Tampa, FL, and will live elsewhere.

This first printing of *An Interface for a Fractal
Landscape* by Ed Steck was printed offset
and bound in an edition of 800 copies by
Thomson-Shore, in Dexter, Michigan.

The design is by Doormouse in collaboration
with the author.

The type is Garamond and Courier.

The cover paper is Mohawk Keaykolour.

Ugly Duckling Presse is a 501(c)(3) nonprofit
small-press publisher and a member of the
Community of Literary Magazines and Presses
(CLMP). We appreciate your support.